The Decorated Home

The Decorated Home

Imaginative Designs and Painting Techniques

Country Homes & Gardens®
New York

Country Homes & Gardens
1271 Avenue of the Americas
New York, NY 10020

Printed in the United States of America

Contents

CHAPTER 1

Imaginative Decorating with Paint

Roller tricks

Professional-looking effects, using a roller tied with string, wire or rubber bands, are easy to master. With just a quick turn of the roller, you can transform plain walls with stylish stripes, checks or multiple patterns in complementary colors.

Creating rough-hewn stripes and checks with a paint roller is quick and simple. You could achieve a more formal striped effect, using accurately measured and spaced strips of masking tape, but your walls would not have the loose, spontaneous look that you can get with a roller. The techniques here are all easy to master, the materials are inexpensive, and rewarding results are surprisingly quick to achieve. You can experiment with different colors and textures to discover a whole new realm of decorative possibilities. Follow the simple steps and learn to create impressive finishes with the humble paint roller—from straightforward stripes to dramatic fake finishes, such as the tiger-stripe look on page 7.

Red dining room

A clever combination of color and texture creates an opulent look for this stylish dining room. Walls striped with red and pink above a plain gray chair rail contrast richly with the color-washing below.

Tan and cream checks

Create this loosely woven check effect by following the steps for stripes and using the rubber band technique. Apply a base coat of rich cream, then apply the check pattern, using a roller and terra-cotta latex paint. Repeat the stripes across a whole wall, then work the roller horizontally, leaving a space one roller's width deep between the stripes.

YOU WILL NEED:
- 1½ quarts flat latex paint in dark red
- 1½ quarts flat latex paint in rose pink
- Standard-size foam paint roller
- 2" paintbrush
- Paint tray
- Flexible tape measure
- Black felt-tip marker
- Chalk
- Plumb line
- Masking tape
- Ball of string
- Scissors
- Clean cloth

There are many exciting and inexpensive decorative effects that you can achieve with a standard foam paint roller and flat latex paint. With a length of string, a twist of florist's wire or a couple of rubber bands fastened around the roller sleeve, you can assemble your own unique tool for creating instant stripes and checks in an endless array of patterns for your own "designer wallpaper."

You can use these techniques on any surface that you would normally decorate with a paint roller, with the added bonus that they require less paint than a solid painted wall. You can use roller techniques also to give a previously decorated wall a quick and instant face-lift.

Color and pattern

Try using a mixture of warm and cool paint shades for contrast and introduce texture, using one of the roller techniques shown here. Choose a complementary color for working the pattern over the base color. You can create a dry, textured look by using the minimum amount of paint on your roller. The size of the pattern you create depends on the width of the roller you use, and the width of the stripes is governed by the spacing between each rubber band or piece of string tied around the

roller. A miniroller, like one used for painting radiators, can create similar patterns on a smaller scale.

Striped walls make a ceiling look higher, whereas checked patterns used in small areas, such as in an alcove or above a chair rail, add interesting decorative detail. A color-washed wall in part of the room may complement a wall that has been roller-striped, particularly when the same tone of paint is used. Adding darker or lighter shades of the same color over existing stripes or checks will create highlights or low-lights and give the whole look more depth.

TIPS

To gain confidence, practice your roller technique on scrap paper before painting a wall. When you are happy that your technique is smooth and steady, you can start painting. Take special care not to press too hard on the roller or the edges will mark the wall. Try to apply the same amount of pressure for each set of stripes so that you create an even, balanced pattern.

Getting started

● If you plan to use roller techniques above a wooden chair rail, decorate this and any abutting door frames or baseboards first, using a paint suitable for woodwork. Before you start, make sure your walls are sound, removing any flaked plaster and filling and sanding any cracks (see page 168). Wash the walls with an all-purpose cleaner, then rinse and dry. Mask off the ceiling and chair rail, using newspaper and masking tape.

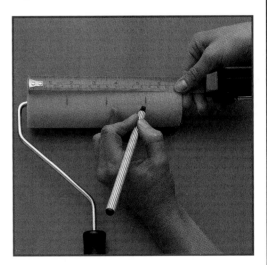

1 Mark the roller

● Before you begin, make sure that your roller is clean and dry and the roller rotates freely. Lay it down on a flat surface and extend the tape measure along the top. Divide the length of the roller by 4; using a light stroke with a felt-tip marker, mark off the halfway point and the quarter measurements on each side. We used a standard-size roller here, but you could use a miniroller for smaller stripes.

● Apply the base coat of deep red latex paint and allow to dry for 2–4 hours. Measure the width across the top of the wall and divide the total width in half. Make a chalk mark at the center point and attach a plumb line with masking tape at this point.

2 Attach the rubber bands

● Holding the roller firmly in your left hand, place one rubber band around the center of the roller sleeve at the position marked. Twist the band on, making sure that it is well embedded in the foam. Secure two more rubber bands in the same way on either side of the center point.

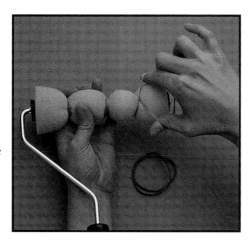

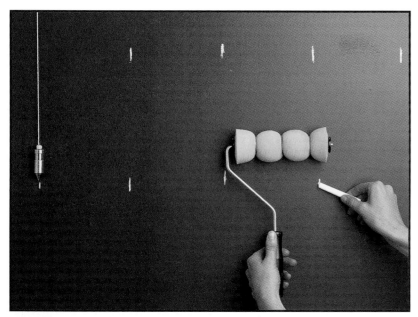

3 Mark the design

● Line up the left side of the roller with the plumb line and make a chalk mark at the right-hand edge of the roller. Repeat across the entire wall, abutting the left side of the roller to the last mark made, marking with chalk as before. Next, using your plumb line as a vertical guide, make chalk marks from the top to the bottom of the wall, keeping the chalk marks parallel with each other. These marks give you a set of guidelines for applying your stripes.

5 Rolling on

● Starting at a mark at the top left of the wall, place the roller at the very top of the wall and draw it downward, using the chalk marks as a guide. Apply more paint to the roller; then, starting one roller's width to the right of the first line, roll a second set of stripes. Continue across the wall in the same way. If your roller runs dry in mid-roll, apply more paint and start again just above where you finished working before.

6 Remove chalk marks

● Once the paint is completely dry, use a soft, clean cloth to rub away the chalk marks. If you have difficulty removing the marks, moisten the cloth very slightly and squeeze it until it is almost dry, then gently work on the remaining chalk marks until they have completely disappeared.

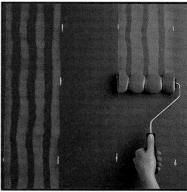

7 Shadows

● To create stripes with low-lights, add some of the red paint you used for the background to the paint tray. Using a brush as before, apply the paint to the roller, working it into the foam. Position the roller exactly over the first stripes made. Using very gentle pressure, draw the roller down so that you apply the paint randomly over the existing stripes. To create highlights, use a lighter pink paint.

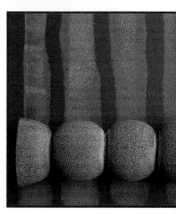

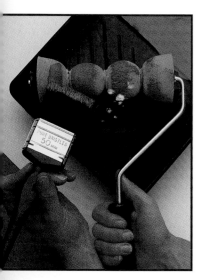

4 Apply the paint

● Pour about 1 cup of the rose pink latex paint into a paint tray. Load the paintbrush with the paint and holding the roller over the tray, brush paint on the roller so that it is well covered on the ridged areas between the rubber bands. Practice rolling the stripes on a piece of scrap paper—if the paint is too thick, dilute it with a little water. Apply each set of practice stripes with a steady hand, using firm, even pressure. Reapply paint to the roller before starting work on the actual wall, and then again at regular intervals as you work.

Tiger stripes

This exotic tiger skin effect is surprisingly easy to achieve—the yellow and orange stripes appear like magic from a roller bound in a spiral, and the black background shows through to provide the "frame" for each square.

Preparation for tiger stripes

The technique

● Apply a base coat of black flat latex paint, then, when dry, mark the wall into roller-width squares, using the chalk method as in step 3 on page 6. Prepare the roller as shown at right. Pour ½ cup each of yellow and orange flat latex paint into the paint tray. Apply the paint to the roller without mixing it to create a two-tone effect. Work the roller down and across alternate squares, lifting it off the wall within the marked squares to leave a bordering frame of black around each one. Continue over the rest of the wall in the same way.

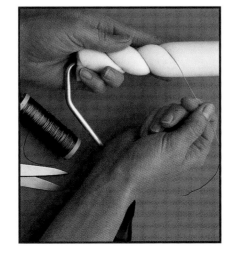

1 Wiring

● Cut a piece of fine wire (such as florist's wire) five times the length of your roller. First, secure the wire to the handle end of the roller. Maintaining an even tension throughout, wind the wire around the roller sleeve five times, keeping roughly the same interval between the spirals.

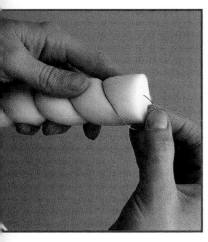

2 Secure the wire end

● Trim the wire, leaving enough length to poke through the center mechanism of the roller. Run the dry roller over a hard surface several times to fix the wire in place. (Instead of wire, you could use thin, strong twine or a length of fishing line. When using these, tie the ends around the roller to fasten them securely.)

TIPS

MINIROLLERS
These are ideal for creating stripes and checks on areas where smaller-scale patterns are more suitable, such as flat-fronted kitchen cabinet doors, backsplashes and bath splashboards.

OVERLOAD ALERT
Roller techniques need only a small amount of paint. If you overload the roller, you will lose the interesting broken texture.

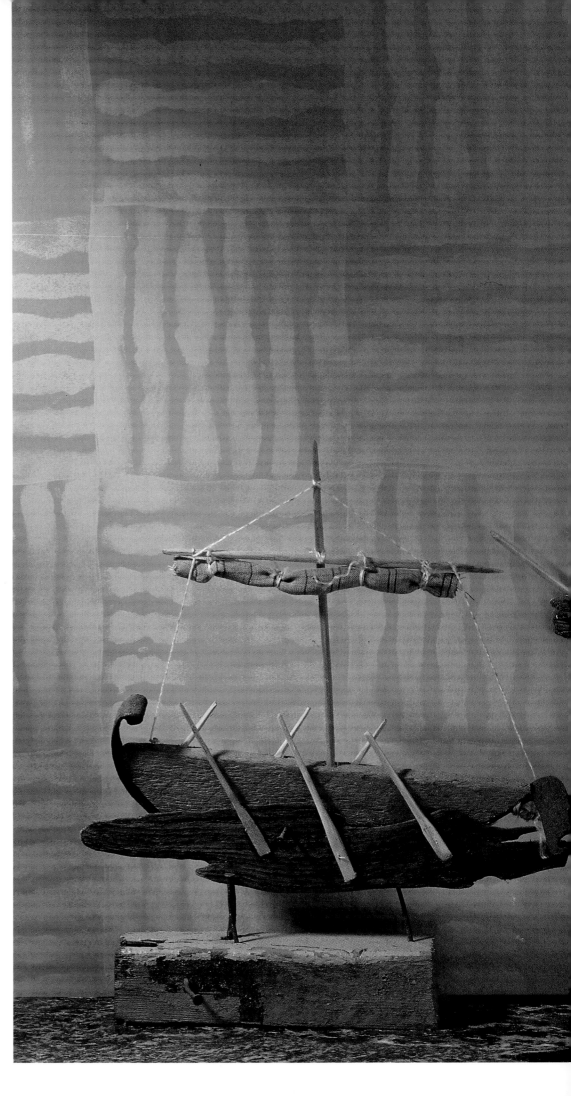

Turquoise checks

Create a spectacular two-tone, checkerboard effect by running a roller horizontally, then vertically across the wall in alternate squares to make an informal geometric pattern. Use a vibrant color combination of two shades of turquoise—colors chosen from the same family are particularly effective for this technique. There is no need to mark guidelines for this effect—you can gauge the squares by eye quite easily. Any irregularities in the size and shape of the squares will simply add to the charm of the finished look.

Preparing the string roller

The technique

● Using a roller or a paintbrush, apply a base coat in dark turquoise latex paint. Pour the light turquoise latex paint into a paint tray, as on page 6, and apply it to the roller, using a 2" paintbrush. Starting along the bottom edge and progressing from left to right, work rows of squares by alternating the roller position from the horizontal to the vertical. Each square will be the width and height of the roller. Reload the roller with paint at regular intervals.

1 Prepare the roller

● Using a felt-tip marker, mark out five spaces along the roller sleeve at equal intervals. Cut five pieces of string into 16" lengths. Tie a piece of string around each of the marked positions, winding each string just once around the roller. This will create a six-stripe roller.

2 Cut off the ends

● Make sure that the string is firmly tied and the knots are well embedded in the foam. Slide the scissor blades down the string and cut the ends away as close to the knot as possible. This will prevent the string marks from appearing on the wall and spoiling the finished effect.

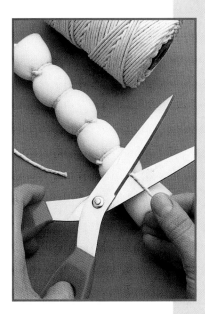

TIPS

■ Always experiment on scrap paper with the tied or wired roller before you start on a project. This gives you the opportunity to alter the intervals between stripes and check that the paint is the right consistency to give you perfect results when you start on the real thing.

■ For a random, abstract pattern, pinch away pieces of foam from a roller with your finger and thumb or a small pair of scissors. Pieces should be no

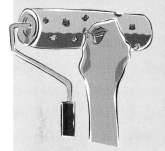

bigger than a marble and no smaller than a pea. Brush the roller with paint and roll over a piece of scrap paper to reveal the pattern.

■ Never skimp on preparation for roller work. If you do not mark adequate guidelines, you can easily slip out of alignment. It is time-consuming if you have to repaint with the background color, then start all over again from scratch.

Design ideas

Create special effects for your walls or furniture by combining color and pattern in unique variations. With roller techniques, you can dramatically change the style of any room—or just an alcove—for a fresh, new look.

Diamonds & stripes

▶ This living room combines two types of roller techniques to great effect. The area below the chair rail was painted in a base coat of blue-gray, then harlequin diamonds were applied freehand in light gray with a miniroller. Above the chair rail, wide stripes of tan were rolled over an oatmeal background with a normal-sized roller "split" in two. For a more subtle look, use different shades of the same color for both the stripe and diamond sections.

Tile style

◀ Mediterranean blue "tiles" were rolled on a plain, off-white background to create the impression of a splashboard in this small bathroom. The area to be "tiled" was marked out, and a miniroller was used to apply a pattern of squares. The slight irregularity of the shapes is reminiscent of handmade tiles and adds to the charm of the effect. Try swirling together two colors, such as golden yellow and green, to create a marbled tile effect.

Latticework

◄ This wall was covered with a background of pale cream, then painted over in pink, using a roller bound in even stripes. First the roller was applied horizontally, then run vertically across the wall to form soft, rough checks. You can create a more dramatic effect with colors that contrast more strongly—or you could roll over the area in a third, complementary shade to create a plaid pattern.

PHOTOGRAPHY BY LIZZIE ORME

Bold lines

► A light color against a dark background creates a bold, distinctive look, perfect for a kitchen, alcove or study. Bright green stripes were rolled on a base of dark green, with the strokes made deliberately uneven to create a rough texture. Try red on yellow, or other contrasting shades, for an even more dramatic look.

Checkerboard

◄ Soft blue and yellow checks were painted alternately on this flea-market table to create a permanent "checkerboard" tablecloth. For a dry-textured effect, roll excess paint from the roller on a piece of paper before starting work on the tabletop.

PHOTOGRAPHY BY SEAN ELLIS

3 Tie the roller

● Wrap rubber bands around the roller between ⅝"–1⅛", 3¼"–3¾" and 5⅞"–6⅜" marks so that they fill these ½"-wide gaps. Next, bind narrow masking tape tightly around the roller between 1¾"–2⅝" and 4⅜"–5¼" marks so that the tape fills these ⅞"-wide gaps.

4 Slice the roller

● Using a craft knife, carefully cut with a gentle sawing action around the roller at each side of the rubber bands and masking tape so that the foam springs back up, protruding above the level of the bound areas.

5 Prepare the tray

● Using the craft knife and metal ruler, cut the cardboard into strips that are ⅞" wide and the length of the roller tray. Using the prepared roller as a guide, place the cardboard strips where the masking tape is wound around the roller. When the strips are in place, use the wider masking tape to secure them to the tray.

YOU WILL NEED:
● **I quart flat latex paint in each of three colors**
● **7" foam roller**
● **Paint tray**
● **Metal ruler**
● **Felt-tip marker**
● **Rubber bands**
● **½"-wide masking tape**
● **I"-wide masking tape**
● **Craft knife**
● **Firm cardboard**
● **Plastic spoons**
The above quantities are sufficient for a 12' x 15' room.

Once you get the knack of creative painting with rollers, there is no limit to the effects you can achieve with the simplest—and cheapest—materials. These three patterns take the technique a step further than the ideas shown on pages 2–11. Just as if selecting a unique designer wallpaper, you can select the colors you want and adapt patterns to suit the style and scale of your room.

Tartan design

The soft tartan effect in this living room is created by rolling vertical and horizontal stripes over a base of blue that has been color-washed over pale lavender. As with all roller techniques, time spent tying the roller sleeve securely is never wasted; one loose knot or stray end of masking tape can easily spoil the effect once you get started.

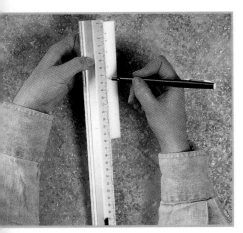

1 Measure the roller

● Using a felt-tip marker, mark the roller at ⅝", 1⅛", 1¾", 2⅝", 3¼", 3¾", 4⅜", 5¼", 5⅞", 6⅜" intervals. Repeat these marks 2 or 3 times around the roller.

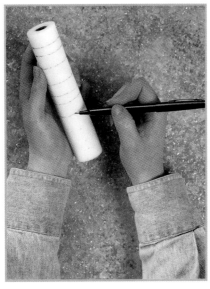

2 Connect the marks

● Connect the sets of marks around the roller to form evenly spaced rings.

6 Prepare the paint

● Mask off the edge of the baseboard from the bottom edge of the wall. Spoon a small amount of one color of latex paint into each section of the roller tray.

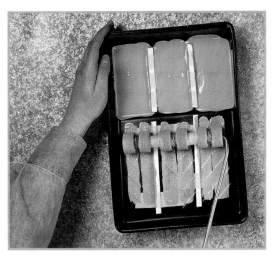

7 Load the roller

● Keeping each pair of ridges in its own color section of the tray, load the roller by rolling it carefully over the channels of paint. Make sure the paint is spread evenly over the foam ridges and roll off any excess in the slanted half of the tray.

8 Vertical stripes

● Starting at one corner of the wall, paint the verticals of the pattern: In one continuous motion, applying an even pressure, push the roller up the wall. You may find it helpful to make occasional pencil marks or chalk marks on the wall to keep your rollered line straight (see Step 3, page 6). Measure 1" from the edge of the first stripe and start the next rolled stripe, leaving this 1" interval. Repeat across the wall, reloading the roller as necessary. Allow to dry completely before adding the horizontals.

● Choose three colors that coordinate well, but use one in a stronger value than the other two to give a more authentic tartan effect. For a softer appearance, use three similar tones of different colors or three different tones of the same color. This is quite a striking effect, so use it as a decoration below a chair rail or in an alcove so that it does not look overpowering.

9 Horizontal stripes

● Loading the paint in the same way, roll the horizontal stripes as for the verticals, starting at the bottom and abutting the baseboard. Leave the same 1"-wide gap between the rolled stripes.

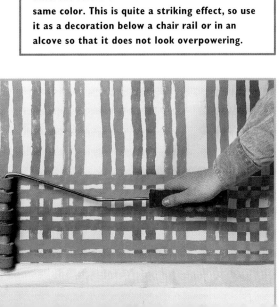

C reate a patterned "roller stamp" to produce a design of abstract shapes where the background shows through. Choose a base color to contrast with the roller color, which is applied in masked stripes across the wall.

Materials

For this technique it is important to use a roller with a solid core. For the sponged background you need very little paint—if you buy two tones of one color, one light and one dark, you could blend a third mid-color from them.

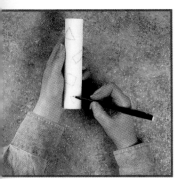

EQUIPMENT

- I quart flat latex paint in pale blue
- Small can of flat latex paint in each of three shades of orange

- 7" foam roller
- Household sponge
- Paint tray
- Felt-tip marker
- Craft knife
- Tape measure
- Pencil
- Plumb line
- 1½"-wide masking tape
- Scissors

2 Cut out the pattern

● Applying firm pressure and using a gentle sawing motion, cut the shapes out of the roller, using a craft knife. You will need to score quite hard to get to the core of the roller. Once at the core of the roller, pull the foam away with your fingers to tear out the base of the shape.

1 Mark the pattern

● Using a felt-tip marker, draw simple shapes at random over the roller surface.

3 Mark the lines

● Mask off the baseboard. Measure along the chair rail or cornice from left to right across the wall and mark at alternating 4" and 5½" intervals. Pencil straight lines down the wall from these points, using a plumb line as a guide.

4 Mask off the stripes

● Working from left to right, position strips of masking tape down the left side of each 4" line and on the right side of the 5½" lines. This will leave revealed alternate 5½"-wide stripes over which you will be painting.

5 Sponge the stripes

● Pour a little of the first sponging color into a tray and using a small wedge of sponge, dab it over the 5½" stripes in random blotches. Repeat over the top with the other two colors.

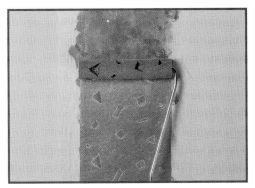

6 Apply the top color

● When the sponged stripes are completely dry, load the roller with blue paint and roll up each sponged stripe in one continuous movement, keeping a steady pressure.

! Immediately after you have loaded the roller with paint but before you start rolling, make sure none of the roller cutouts are clogged with paint, or these will not produce a pattern.

One foam roller tightly bound with string and a miniroller are the basis for this close-textured vertical stripe and zigzag border. Keep the look simple by using just two colors—a bright color rolled over a light background.

REQUIREMENTS

● I quart flat latex paint in bright blue
● 7" foam roller
● Foam miniroller
● Paint tray
● String
● Scissors
● Tape measure
● Pencil
● 1½"-wide masking tape

1 Stringing the roller

● Wind the string tightly around the large roller sleeve, leaving small gaps between each wind. Secure the ends inside the roller with masking tape.

2 Mark the wall

● Measuring up from the baseboard, use a pencil to mark two points 38" and 42" up from the floor. Repeat at regular intervals all around the room. The space between these two points will be the width of the border.

3 Mask off the border

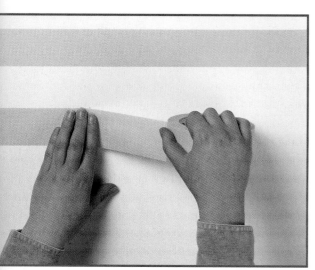

● Apply the wide masking tape along the top of the 42" marks all around the room. Apply a second strip of tape below the 38" marks. The rolled effect will start below the lower strip of tape. Mask off the baseboard.

4 Roll on the paint

● Pour enough blue latex paint into the tray to cover the base coat generously. Load the bound roller with paint, wipe away any excess and roll up the wall in straight continuous lines. Keep a firm pressure at all times and reload the roller with paint when necessary.

5 Remask the border

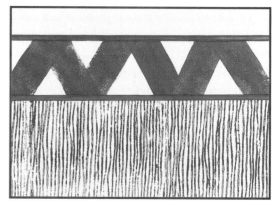

● When the rolled paint is dry, peel away the lower strip of masking tape. Place a strip of wide masking tape to mask off the top of the top edge of the rollered pattern. To avoid it lifting off the paintwork, it may help to de-tack the tape on a piece of material before applying it to the wall.

TIPS

■ After the roller has had a lot of use or if it dries with paint on it, the string will become embedded in the foam. This prevents the roller from moving smoothly. To avoid this, try to work on a project until it is finished. Wipe the edges of the roller frequently to avoid clogging and smearing.

■ If your paintwork is clean and in good condition, and if you are happy with the existing color as a background, you may not need to repaint the whole room. However, if you want a complete face-lift, select a new color for the background.

■ If roller marks show beyond the masking tape, touch up with the base color when dry.

6 Zigzag border

● Load the miniroller with paint and roll a zigzag border along the masked area. If you are not confident, mark off intervals with a pencil as a guide.

7 Add molding

● Remove all the masking tape. Measure lengths of molding to fit the room. Dilute blue paint with a little water and sponge over the molding. When the paint is dry, apply the molding to the wall above and below the border.

Mosaic stamping

You do not need to spend a lot of money on expensive tiling to give your home a look of the Mediterranean. With just a few tools and a little paint, you can transform plain walls with versatile mosaic patterns.

Bring a splash of color to a dull room in no time with stamped mosaic patterns, which are fun to create, using inexpensive materials such as sponge sheets and latex paint.

Before you begin the mosaic, prepare your walls by giving them a coat of pale yellow flat latex paint, followed by a very light color wash of terra-cotta. Allow to dry for two to four hours, then start marking the guidelines for the mosaic stamping. As with any paint technique that is worked along straight lines, proper preparation is important so that the stamped images are properly aligned and you do not compound an error as you work. Either follow the design and colors used in the steps below, or use your imagination to create your own unique designs to suit your decor.

YOU WILL NEED:
- Small cans of flat latex paint in pale blue, lavender, mint green, orange, burnt orange
- Small paintbrushes
- Several sponge sheets
- Metal ruler
- Felt-tip marker
- Scissors
- White glue
- Firm cardboard
- Masking tape
- Craft knife
- Cutting mat
- String
- Plumb line
- Spirit level
- Pencil
- Plain white paper
- Soft eraser

1 Measure and mark

- Measure, then mark about fifty ⅞" squares on the rough side of the sponge sheets, using a metal ruler. Mark the lines firmly with a felt-tip marker.

2 Cut and lay out

- Cut out the sponge sheet squares, using sharp scissors.
- Glue the squares smooth side up ⅛" apart on a piece of cardboard, using white glue. Make two blocks of 5" x 5" squares. When set, trim away the excess cardboard.

5 Trim off excess

● When the glue is firmly set, cut away excess cardboard, using a craft knife on a cutting mat. Hold the circle firmly in place so that the craft knife does not slip and cut the sponge "tiles."

4 Cut shapes

● Cut the circle out; divide it into random angular shapes. Using white glue, glue the pieces in place smooth side down on a piece of cardboard, leaving uniform ⅛" gaps between pieces, so that the pieces form a round shape.

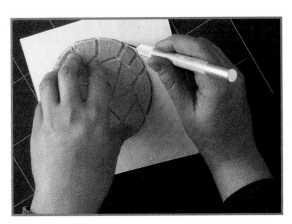

6 Measure the wall

3 Draw a circle

● Using a felt-tip marker, draw a circle on the rough side of a sponge sheet, using the inside of a roll of masking tape as a guide—this will create the circular stamp for the round motifs.

! Remember that once cut up and reconstructed, any shape you draw will be bigger because of the gaps between the cutouts. If you would like a shape to fill a specific space, cut the cardboard first, then cut the sponge to fit it, rather than the other way around.

● Attach the end of a piece of string to one end of the wall. Using a spirit level to ensure that the line will be level, stretch the string out along the wall and tape the other end to the wall with masking tape to create a guide for stamping.

● Using a ruler and pencil, measure along the string and make a mark on the wall every 16", about ⅝" above the line of the piece of string.

19

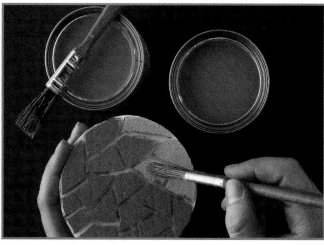

Stamp a kitchen utensil hanger with bright, stylized pink roses set in small blue squares on a background of pale yellow.

7 Load the circle

brushes. Cover roughly half of the mosaic pieces with orange paint and the other half with burnt orange. Be careful not to overlap the two colors on any one "tile" as this will spoil the effect. If you find it easier, use a piece of paper to mask one area while you load the other with paint.

● Lightly stamp the circle to leave a print on a piece of plain

● Load the mosaic circle with two shades of orange paint, using two small

paper. This will remove any excess paint and also help to prevent paint from smudging the outlines of the mosaic. Set this print aside to use later as a mask when over-printing (see step 9).

9 Squares

● Load the square sponge tiles on one stamp in lines of alternating green, lavender and blue paint; blot off any excess paint on plain paper. Using the string as a guide, stamp along the wall, continuing over the taped paper circles. Make sure you keep the edge of the square stamp level with the string. Allow the mosaic stamping to dry, then carefully remove the taped paper circles.

8 Stamp the wall

● Stamp the circle on the the wall ⅝" above the string over one of the pencil marks. Press firmly in the middle and around the edges. Repeat along the wall at each mark, reloading with paint as necessary.

● While the wall stamps

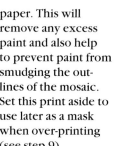

are drying, cut out several outlines of the test circle on plain paper, leaving a ⅛" border around the edge. Make double loops of masking tape and use to stick the paper circles over the dry stamped circles on the wall, masking them completely.

10 Sun template

● To make a stamp for the central sun motif, draw around the outside of the roll of masking tape on the rough side of a sponge sheet. Cut this out, then cut in irregular shapes, as for the smaller circle. Glue back in shape on a piece of

cardboard, allowing a uniform ⅛" gap between the pieces.
● Using a ruler and felt-tip marker, draw a tapering zigzag shape to represent one of the sun's rays on the rough side of a piece of sponge sheet. Keep the length of the ray to about three-quarters of the diameter of the main round sun template.

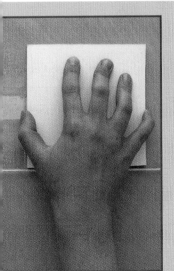

11 Sunray stamp

● Cut the zigzag shape into three or four irregular pieces to create a mosaic effect. Glue these onto a piece of cardboard, using white glue and leaving the same gaps of about ⅛" between the pieces.

12 Smaller sunray stamp

● Referring to steps 10 and 11, create a stamp for making a smaller zigzag sunray. This will form the smaller rays of the sun between the larger stamped zigzags. When the pieces are firmly glued in place, trim away excess cardboard from around the edges, using a craft knife on a cutting board.

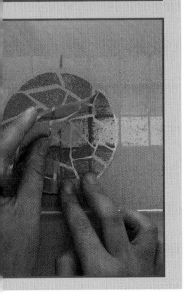

13 Stamp zigzags

● Load the large circle stamp and bigger zigzag stamps with paint, then print on plain paper in the desired shape. (There is no need to add the smaller zigzags at this stage.) Cut out roughly and place the paper template on the wall, making pencil marks around the circle as a guide.

14 Stamp sun motifs

● Reload the circle with two shades of orange paint, using two brushes. Using the pencil marks as a guide, stamp onto the wall, pressing firmly in the middle and at the edges. Stamp the larger zigzag at the top, bottom and sides of the circle, then stamp smaller zigzags in between them.

Mosaic frame

This wide frame, with its circular mosaic pattern, is reminiscent of paving stones. A garden mood is created with gold "stones" stamped on dark green to complement the bright colors of the yellow-and-black bird among the red flowers.

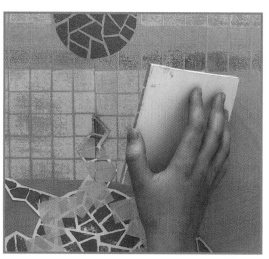

15 Mask off motif

● While the central motif is drying, cut out an outline of the imprint and four small zigzag pieces on plain paper, leaving a ⅛" border all around each one. Mask off the stamped motif on the wall as in step 8, using extra masking tape to ensure that the area between the circle and each zigzag is completely covered.

16 Stamp squares

● Load the second block of mosaic sponge squares with the pale blue paint and stamp all over the central area over and around the masked sun motif, working from left to right and top to bottom. Allow to dry before removing the taped paper sun motifs. Erase any pencil marks that are visible, using a soft eraser.

Graffiti
PATTERNS

Create your own unique designs with this easy-to-master freehand paint technique. Using sweeping brushstrokes and a paint roller, you can make a distinctive pattern in any size and color you choose.

YOU WILL NEED:
- 1 quart flat latex paint in aqua green
- 8 oz flat latex paint in white, dark green and terra-cotta
- Liquid leaf in gold
- Paint thinner
- Large and medium-sized paintbrushes
- Textured foam roller
- Short-bristled and medium-sized artist's brushes
- Roller tray
- Four paint pails
- Measuring cup
- Mixing sticks
- Tape measure
- Pencil and soft eraser
- Ruler
- Brown paper
- Plain white paper

Bold, abstract freehand designs, painted graffiti-style on a contrasting background color, bring a unique look to any room and yet are surprisingly easy to create. You do not need to be a skilled artist—just use the texture of simple sweeping brushstrokes to create a base for an easily built-up pattern. The materials and colors you select can make simple patterns look striking—there is no need to choose motifs that are elaborate or difficult to copy.

You can use purely abstract designs, made up of straight lines or curves used together in colors that blend, or you can choose shapes that suggest elements from the room you are decorating—shell-like swirls or waves for a bathroom; smaller, petal-shaped patterns for a porch or garden room.

Materials

Graffiti patterns work best if you use a color wash for all the various swirls and lines, as this lets the brushstrokes show clearly. To recreate the bathroom shown here, use a color wash as your base coat and paint the graffiti—with the exception of the gold liquid leaf lines—in flat latex paint diluted with approximately twice as much water. You can texture a foam roller by pinching out small circles with your thumb and forefinger to create a loose, spongy pattern.

1 Mix the color wash

● Pour the aqua flat latex paint into a paint pail and dilute it with three times as much water. Add the water a little at a time, stirring continuously.

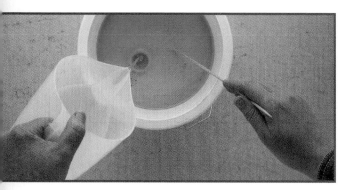

2 Paint the base coat

● Use the large paintbrush to cover the area above the shelf or chair rail with the aqua wash. Use large brushstrokes and work the paint in a crisscross pattern. Allow to dry for 2–4 hours.

3 Measure the border

● Using tape measure and pencil, mark the wall 2¾" up from the shelf and in from the window. Using the ruler and pencil, join the points into a line. Measure 6 ¼" up from this and draw a second line.

4 Mix the graffiti colors

● Pour the white, dark green and terra-cotta flat latex paint into separate paint pails. Dilute each with twice as much water, adding a little at a time and stirring continuously.

5 Paint graffiti waves

● Using the medium-sized paintbrush and white color wash, apply the first graffiti marks. Work from left to right inside the penciled guidelines. Brush the wash on in single, sweeping curved strokes. Allow to dry for 2–4 hours.

8 Apply second graffiti marks

● Using the short-bristled artist's brush and terra-cotta color wash, paint thin stripes randomly over the roller marks. Allow to dry.

6 Practice roller graffiti

● Pour the dark green color wash into the roller tray. Load the roller with paint, then remove the excess by rolling it on brown paper. On the plain paper, practice rolling graffiti marks using short, light strokes.

7 Apply roller graffiti

● Load the roller with dark green color wash and roll off the excess on brown paper. Starting on the left, place the roller at the top of the first graffiti marks and roll over them, working downward in short strokes. Keep the pressure light and even throughout. Allow to dry.

TIPS

■ If you don't have a chair rail for your graffiti pattern to follow, you can draw a mock one, using string and chalk, and paint a faux border.

■ Use a soft-lead pencil or colored chalk for drawing in your guidelines so that the marks are easy to remove.

■ For the textured roller graffiti marks, use short, quick "nudges" rather than long strokes.

■ If your bathroom fixtures are chrome, use silver liquid leaf instead of gold to apply the final layer of graffiti marks.

Create a coordinated look with graffiti-painted accessories. The technique is easy to use on cushions and curtains—choose fabric paints in colors that blend or contrast with your graffiti border. Keep the look simple, picking out elements from your original design.

9 Apply gold leaf

● Starting on the left side and using light brushstrokes, use the medium-sized artist's brush to paint thin lines of gold liquid leaf over the graffiti. If the gold liquid leaf is too thick, or for light touches of gold, dilute it with a little paint thinner.

10 Remove pencil marks

● Use a soft eraser to remove the pencil guidelines. Be careful not to press too hard, or you could lift off some of the pattern.

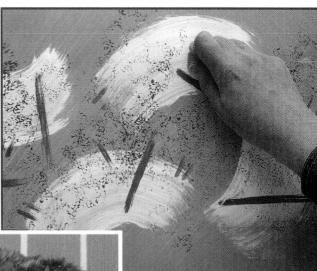

Graffiti wooden toy box

Graffiti is an ideal paint technique for a child's room— use bold designs in bright primary colors to complement toys of all shades, shapes and sizes. Here, a plain painted wooden toy box was transformed with a large yellow, green and red graffiti pattern. The first brushed marks are in yellow color wash, then a textured roller is used over the top. The lines of green and red—also color washes—were added, using a small paintbrush.

For a coordinated look, repeat the design as a border on walls or use a scaled-down version on chairs, desks and tables. Graffiti patterns are also easy to apply to fabrics— use fabric paint in bright colors on bed linen, remembering to follow the manufacturer's instructions.

COMBING

Use the comb edges of a graining tool and discover how quickly a simple combing technique can transform anything—from a wall to a storage chest.

The technique of combing is simple—and it is easy to correct, fun to experiment with and offers endless possibilities of patterns and color combinations. The theory is very straightforward. You paint a colored glaze over a background of oil-based paint, and while the glaze is still wet, comb it away to leave a pattern in the two colors.

Equipment

Start with a background color in an oil-based paint. It is important to use a paint with a flat finish—a gloss paint would be too shiny for the glaze to adhere to. For the combed layer, you need oil-based glaze, which is available from paint stores; paint thinner to dilute the glaze; and artist's oil color, which comes in tubes of about 1.25 oz from art supply shops. (You will find that a little oil color goes a very long way, so one tube will last for several different projects.) Finally, you will need a graining comb. We have used the combing▶

GRAHAM RAE

29

edges of a rocker-type graining tool to give two contrasting patterns, but you can use metal, rubber or plastic combs, which are available from craft shops, or make your own out of firm cardboard.

Patterns and practice

Follow the step-by-step instructions and experiment with patterns and the effects you can get with different combs. The glaze stays workable for up to 20 minutes after you brush it on, so you can keep on repainting and combing until you find just the right pattern to give your home a really individual and personal look.

Before you begin, prepare and paint the surface that you want to comb with oil-based paint in your chosen color and allow it to dry for at least 16 hours. Assemble your equipment, as shown below, with plenty of paper towels or rags for wiping your comb—and you are ready to start.

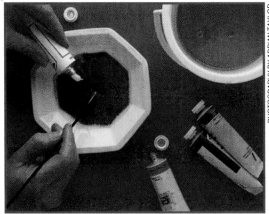

PHOTOGRAPHY BY ADRIAN TAYLOR

1 Mix the glaze

● Place a little artist's oil color in a saucer and add a little paint thinner. Mix well, then stir into the glaze in a paint pail. Make sure you mix enough colored glaze to complete the whole job, as exact colors are hard to match. The glaze should be the consistency of thin cream, so dilute with paint thinner as necessary.

! When the paper towels or cloths that you use for wiping your comb get saturated with glaze, spread the pieces out to dry where the air can circulate freely around them. Oil-based glaze is very combustible; if cloths are left to dry crumbled up in a confined space, they could ignite.

2 Preparation

● Brush the colored glaze thinly over the base color, spreading it so that the cover is even. You need to comb the glaze while it is fresh, so only cover an area about 8" wide to the full depth of the area to be combed and finish with even vertical strokes, leaving as few brushmarks as possible.

YOU WILL NEED:
● I quart flat oil-based paint in white
● Artist's oil colors in yellow and light green or other chosen colors
● I quart oil-based glaze
● Paint thinner
● 3" paintbrush or roller and tray
● 2" paintbrush
● Graining comb or two 3"-wide homemade cardboard combs with even ⅛"- and ¹⁄₁₆"- wide teeth
● Saucer
● Paint pail
● Plumb line
● Paper towels or cloth for cleaning
The quantities above are sufficient to paint and comb the area below a mid-wall chair rail in a hall measuring 6' x 12'.

GRAHAM RAE

4 The first combed line

● Holding the wide-toothed comb at arm's length and starting immediately below the rail, draw the comb down to the baseboard in one continuous stroke next to the plumb line.

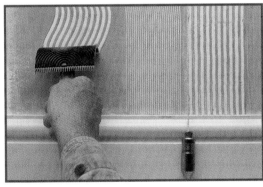

5 The second combed line

● Working either to the right or left of your first combed line, draw the fine edge of the comb down the wet glaze next to the thick stripes.

6 Wavy lines

● Reposition the plumb line as you work and continue painting on glaze so that you are always working on a freshly brushed strip. Wipe excess glaze from the wide-toothed comb; leaving a gap of about ½" after the previous straight line, comb in an even wiggle down the wall.

7 Clean the baseboard

● Do not worry if you leave blotches of glaze on the baseboard. Wipe any smudges away while the glaze is still wet, using a cloth dampened with a little paint thinner.

For a first combing project, choose a half-wall, such as the area below a chair rail. As you get more experienced, you can tackle longer combing on whole walls.

3 Attach a plumb line

● To make sure that you comb in a straight line, attach a plumb line to the chair rail about 4" from where you want to make your first stroke of the comb. If you attach the line with a small piece of reusable adhesive, you can move it along as you comb each strip to be sure of keeping your lines perfectly vertical.

HELP FILE

■ Whatever mistake you make in combing, it is always easy to correct. Use your paintbrush to redistribute the glaze, then start again. If you need to, you can refresh the glaze several times until you are satisfied.

■ If you apply the glaze too thickly, your combing may look blobby. To correct this, use a brush to take off some of the glaze and start again.

SURFACES
You can comb over any smooth surface that can be treated with oil-based paint. For surfaces such as laminates, rub down, prime and paint, then comb as in the steps.

DRYING TIME
Allow at least 16 hours for oil-based glaze to dry.

● Graining combs are available in metal, rubber or plastic, with a wide variety of different tooth patterns. To make your own, see Tips, page 32.

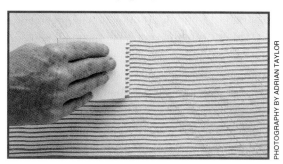

1 Paint the unfinished wood with a coat of primer; allow to dry. Next, paint the drawers with pink satin-finish oil-based paint; allow to dry. For a cloudy effect, dilute a different shade of pink with paint thinner and sponge in patches over the dry base. Mix white artist's oil color with paint thinner and glaze (about 20 oz), as on page 30, and paint over the dry sponged base color.

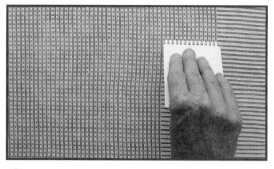

PHOTOGRAPHY BY ADRIAN TAYLOR

2 Using a comb with very fine teeth, draw it across the glaze in horizontal lines, abutting each stroke of the comb closely with the one before. Wipe the comb clean between strokes.

SEAN ELLIS

Combed chest

A plain, unfinished wood storage chest gets a new lease on life with a coat of pink paint and easy crisscross combing in white.

3 While the glaze is still wet, use the same comb to make abutting, vertical lines through the existing horizontal pattern. This creates a fine, almost fabriclike, woven effect. Repeat the whole process on all surfaces of the chest and drawers.

TIPS

IMPROVISED COMBS

A homemade cardboard comb will last for one or two projects, but will soon lose the sharpness on its teeth. For a much longer-lasting comb, use an out-of-date credit card or the soft, rubbery edge of a car windshield wiper. You can also get interesting effects using wide-toothed hair combs or the combs supplied with tile adhesive.

PAINT CHOICE

Oil-based paint can take 16 hours to dry, so for a quicker-drying background paint, use acrylic paint. This is a water-based paint that dries to give the same effect as the oil-based variety, but takes as little as four hours before you can work over it.

Cutting a comb

● To make your own comb, cut a piece of firm cardboard or plastic the desired width and about 2½" deep. With a ruler, mark off even teeth at intervals along the combing edge; cut with sharp scissors or a craft knife, making sure that the gaps and teeth are even, respectively, for a uniform effect.

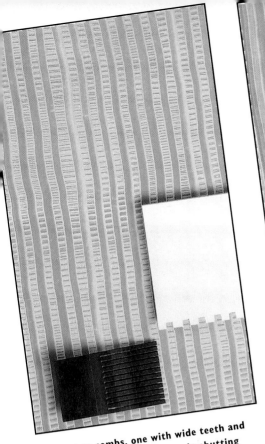

● Use two combs, one with wide teeth and one with fine teeth. Draw closely abutting horizontal lines with the fine comb and use the wide-toothed comb vertically on top.

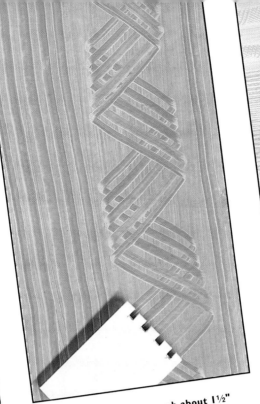

● With a wide-toothed comb about 1½" wide, draw straight lines 2" apart. Hold the comb with the teeth parallel to the lines and draw a zigzag line in between the lines.

● Use a wide, fine comb to draw straight lines about 2¾" apart. In the spaces, hold a thin, fine comb with the teeth parallel to the lines and draw two small zigzag lines.

Combing patterns

Use combs in different textures and widths to create fascinating, almost 3-D patterns—use your imagination for subtle and eye-catching color mixes.

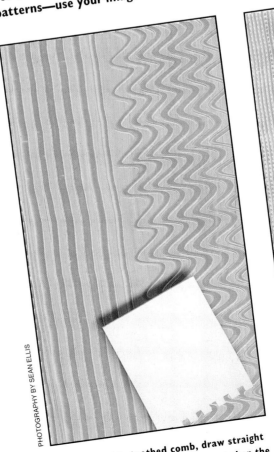

● A very fine comb gives a subtle effect that looks like closely woven fabric; the pattern is made more delicate if combed in plain white glaze, as shown, which allows the pink to show through. For some unusual effects with plain combing, experiment with multicolored and shaded backgrounds.

● Using a wide-toothed comb, draw straight lines that are about 1¼" wider apart than the comb. Hold the teeth at right angles to the lines and draw a wiggly line in the spaces.

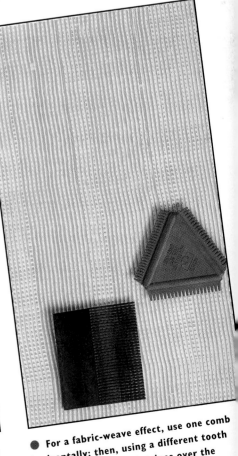

● For a fabric-weave effect, use one comb horizontally; then, using a different tooth pattern, comb vertical stripes over the top while the glaze is still wet.

EQUIPMENT

YOU WILL NEED:
- 2½ quarts flat latex paint in lilac
- 1–2 quarts acrylic glaze
- 1 quart flat latex paint in terra-cotta and blue
- Small and medium-sized paintbrushes
- Graining comb
- Rocker-type graining tool
- Masking tape
- Scissors
- Two paint pails
- Plastic spoons
- Mixing sticks
- Tape measure
- Set square
- Pencil
- Large sheet of cardboard
- Craft knife
- Cutting board
- Ruler
- Chalk
- Plumb line
- Lint-free cloths
- Ceramic mixing bowl

Advanced Combing

Combing will transform anything that has a flat surface, such as walls, doors and floors, and add color and interest to plain furniture. It can be used to create a subtle, sophisticated effect with two pale shades that blend together, or a dramatic finish with bright, bold, contrasting colors.

You can take the combing technique a step further (see basic Combing, pages 30-31) by using an acrylic glaze, tinted with latex paint, along with a series of cardboard templates that you can trace on your surface to create a striking geometric design.

Getting started

If you intend to use the combing technique on a specific area of a wall (above or below a chair rail or on panels, for instance), make a rough sketch of your room on paper first. This will help with the placement of any combed sections and will give you a good idea of how a geometric design will work.

Once you have selected and mixed your colors, try them out on a piece of scrap cardboard to see how they work with one another. If the result is not to your liking, you can darken or dilute the glaze or alter the color you have chosen for your background paint.

1 Apply the base coat

● Sand any loose paint on the wall and wipe to remove grease and dirt. Mask the chair rail on both sides. Apply the base coat of lilac latex paint to the wall above and below the chair rail.

2 Mix the glazes

● Pour the acrylic glaze into two paint pails, adding twice as much to one. Add terra-cotta to the pail with the least glaze until you get the shade you want. Repeat for the blue.

3 Draw the squares

● For the zigzag template, draw two 44"-long parallel lines 4¼" apart on the cardboard to make a column. Leave a 2⅜" gap and repeat. Divide into squares by adding horizontal lines at 4¼" intervals.

35

4 Draw the zigzags

● Once you have divided your columns into squares, draw a line diagonally across the first square from top right to bottom left. Then draw a line in the square underneath from top left to bottom right and so on. This will make a zigzag pattern. Repeat for your second column of squares. Cut along the zigzag lines. Cut a 5⅛" square for your diamond template.

5 Mark the template positions

● Mark your starting point at the top and bottom of the wall, using the plumb line to ensure that your chalk marks align. Measure 20" from this point and mark at the top and bottom of the wall. Then measure 11" and mark again. Repeat across the entire wall.

6 Draw around the zigzag template

● Place the template on the wall, using your first set of marks as a guide for the left-hand edge. Draw around it using the chalk. Tape the template into position on the chair rail and at the base of the wall, but take care not to remove any chalk marks.

 If you apply the glaze too thickly, your combing will be uneven. If this happens, brush away some of the glaze and start again.

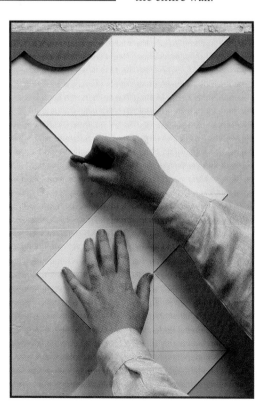

7 Flip over and draw around

● Flip the template over, line up the right-hand edge with the first 20" mark and draw around it. Flip the template back, line up with the 11" mark and draw around it. Flip the template over and then line up with the next mark. Continue until you have filled the entire area.

8 Draw around the diamond template

● Center the diamond template in one of the gaps between the zigzags; draw around it. Repeat for all the gaps. Position the diamonds by eye, but use the plumb line to make sure they are straight.

9 Mask off outlines

● Mask between your zigzag and diamond shapes, taping inside all the pencil guidelines and making sure you cover the spaces between the shapes completely. Mask off carefully, using several strips of tape over one area, if necessary, to give neat, straight edges.

TIPS

■ Wipe the comb clean between strokes to avoid a buildup of glaze. Don't wait until the comb has clogged, as dried glaze is hard to remove.

■ You can use all kinds of household objects to create a design when combing in bold patterns. A paper plate, for example, makes an ideal template for circular patterns. If you choose a curved object, use flexible tape to mask off your guidelines.

■ If you are combing in a solid color on a large section of wall, apply the glaze section by section in vertical stripes. Comb each section immediately after you have applied the glaze. This will help to prevent the wall from drying before you have finished combing your pattern.

■ As the glaze is water-based, you can wipe away any stray smudges with a damp cloth.

10 Comb the zigzags

● Apply the blue glaze mixture inside the masked-off zigzag areas, working on one section at a time to ensure the glaze does not dry before you have finished combing. Brush glaze all the way down one-half of the zigzag and then comb in straight lines. Draw the comb down in one continuous stroke. Repeat, always working in sections.

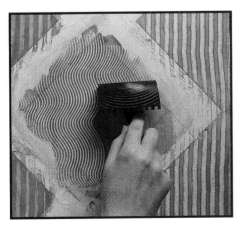

11 Comb the diamonds

● Make sure that the blue zigzags are dry to the touch, then brush the terra-cotta glaze inside the masked-off diamond areas. Use the graining tool and comb in wavy lines. For maximum contrast, make these lines finer and closer together than the straight lines of the zigzags, with less of the base color showing through.

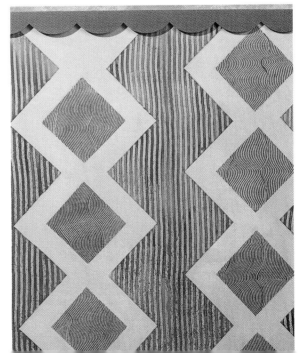

Geometric tabletop

Give an old-fashioned table a hi-tech look with simple combing.

This attractive combed design gives an old table a new lease on life. The simple tones of cream and black combine well with almost any modern decorating scheme.

To create the look, paint the base of the table in flat black latex paint and paint the tabletop a rich cream color. Using a tape measure and fine-lead pencil, locate and mark the center point of the table. Draw a straight line across the diameter, followed by two diagonal lines to divide the table into six equal portions. Connect the pencil lines at the table edge to form three alternating triangles. With masking tape (and paper, if necessary), mask a neat line around the outside of each triangle, making sure each apex is clearly defined. Cover the triangles with flat black-tinted acrylic glaze, then comb horizontally from the base of each triangle. Allow to dry for four hours, then apply two coats of flat acrylic varnish for a durable and hard-wearing finish.

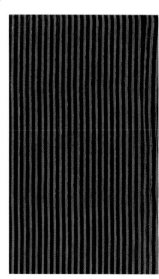

Before

Color guide

● For a fresh look, comb sea green over bright lemon yellow.

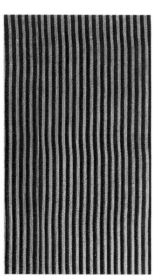

● To get a luxurious finish, comb deep purple over gold.

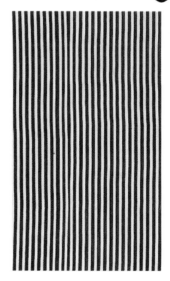

● Create a three-dimensional effect with red and white.

● Use shades of blue for this warm Mediterranean look.

Ways with MOLDINGS

Baseboard, coving, chair rails and other trim can be given a creative treatment in just the same way as a wall. Get inspired by these quick and creative ideas and give a little lift to the moldings in your home.

Freehand and stamped designs

Coordinate plain interior trim with a painted border at chair rail height, using freehand patterns with simple stamped details. A chair rail is a perfect device for splitting a tall wall and allowing you scope to decorate the upper and lower areas of a room with different effects. If you don't have one, create one as described here and include it in your decorating scheme.

For an unusual wall texture, coat the lower wall with deep red flat latex paint and before it is dry, scrub lightly at random with a scouring sponge.

EQUIPMENT

YOU WILL NEED:

- 16 oz flat latex paint in dull plummy (dark) brown and soft brown
- 8 oz flat latex paint in aqua
- Two medium-sized paintbrushes
- Fine artist's brush
- Tape measure
- Pencil
- Ruler
- Masking tape
- Scissors
- Measuring cup
- Plastic plates or palette
- Felt-tip marker
- Craft knife
- Stiff cardboard
- Cutting mat
- Household sponge

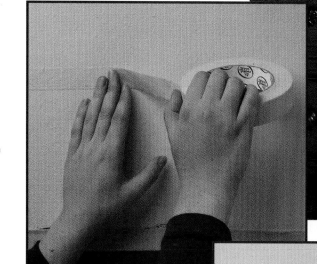

1 Masking off

- Measuring up from the floor, make pencil marks at 40" (the top of the painted area) and 48". Repeat around the room. Join the horizontal marks, then run masking tape above the top line and below the bottom line.

2 Paint the "rail"

- Apply dark brown latex paint in horizontal strokes to the masked-off area. Before it dries, dilute some soft brown latex paint with water and brush over the top. Allow to dry.

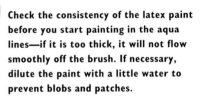

4 Paint in the design

● Cut an 8½"-long rectangle from cardboard, making sure the corners are perfect right angles. Placing the cardboard at an angle, draw a line starting at the top left pencil mark and going to the second mark at the bottom of the rail, then draw another line parallel to the first line but starting ½" in from the top. Using the artist's brush and the aqua paint, paint over the pencil lines.

● Repeat the procedure all around the room. Then, starting at the bottom left mark on the chair rail, work in the same way to build up a crisscross lattice of parallel lines all around the rail.

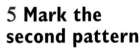

Check the consistency of the latex paint before you start painting in the aqua lines—if it is too thick, it will not flow smoothly off the brush. If necessary, dilute the paint with a little water to prevent blobs and patches.

5 Mark the second pattern

● Measure the width of the door trim (or baseboard, if it is narrower), and cut a cardboard square with a diagonal the same width. Mark in pencil at 6" intervals along each edge of the baseboard and trim. Place the square template with a corner on each mark and draw around it.

● Use the artist's brush and aqua paint to outline the squares. Add parallel lines, crossing at the corners inside the outline.

3 Plan the pattern

● Starting at one corner, measure along the top and bottom of the painted chair rail, making pencil marks at 6" intervals all around the room.

6 Stamped patterns

● On a piece of sponge, draw a circle a little smaller than the center of the square shape; cut away the surrounding sponge. Pick up a little aqua paint, dab off the excess and use to stamp a circle in the center of each lined square.

Trompe l'oeil sky

Create the impression of a room with its ceiling open to the sky and the walls topped with elegant pillars—all done with a simple combination of color-sponging and stenciling.

The more experienced you get, the more ambitious you can be with your creative paint ideas. Start with a white base and experiment with colors, techniques and textures to get the look of windswept clouds. If you are not happy with the effect, simply add more color or wait until the paint is dry and work over the problem area with a lighter color.

1 Prepare the background

● Mask off the picture rail and cornice. Pour a little gray-blue latex paint into a plastic plate; use a sea sponge to spread on the paint, creating an uneven texture. When dry, sponge on the blue paints, mixing them to get varied tones and working in random patches for a patchy effect. Allow to dry. Repeat over the whole ceiling.

4 Stencil the pillars

● Position the stencil on the first pair of marks; check to see that it is perfectly perpendicular, using the set square, then secure with masking tape. Stencil in the lightened beige. Repeat over the pairs of pencil marks around the room.

2 Sponge on the clouds

● Pour a little white latex paint into a plate, then use the second sponge to add patchy clouds, working in a circular motion to give an impression of movement. Remove the masking tape when dry.

5 Adding shadows

● When the stenciling is dry, use the artist's brush and the darker beige latex paint to paint over the thin detail of the stencil twists to give a shadowed effect.

Although you need to give a solid cover to the stenciling, make sure you do not pick up too much latex paint on the sponge, or it will bleed. If you prefer, use acrylic stencil paint in pale beige for this stage—it is easier to use and dries more quickly.

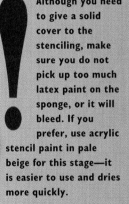

3 Mark the pillars

● Starting at one corner, make corresponding pencil marks at 9½" intervals along the bottom of the cornice and the top of the picture rail. Extend the border stencil to the height of the sky panel.

6 Paint the cornice

● Mask off the painted sky area, then paint the cornice and picture rail, using the lightened beige paint. Allow to dry; then remove the tape.

Cat and mouse baseboard

Add a clever touch to a plain wall with an embellished stencil decoration of a cat guarding a trompe l'oeil mousehole from atop a pile of books. The possibilities are endless if you use other designs from The Stencil Collection, such as the flower posy or wreath. Use a photocopier to enlarge the stencil to give your chosen motif more impact.

YOU WILL NEED:

- Sitting cat stencil from The Stencil Collection
- Artist's watercolors
- Water-based stencil paints in beige, gray, red and black
- Fine artist's brush
- Gold and silver pens
- Household sponge
- Ruler
- Pencil and pen
- Masking tape
- Scissors
- Mixing bowl
- Stencil acetate
- Craft knife
- Cutting mat
- Plain paper
- Compass
- Soft eraser

1 Plan the pile of books

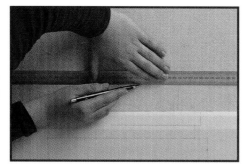

- Working up from floor level, draw four or five rectangles of varying sizes on top of each other to represent book spines.

2 Add color

- Mask off the carpet, then color in the book spines in watercolors, shading to add realism. Allow to dry.

3 Adding details

- Use the gold and silver pens to add detail to the book spines, writing in titles and adding some decorative trimmings.

■ To add interest to moldings, paint in white oil-based paint; when dry, brush with colored oil glaze, working into the detailing. Stipple over to remove the brushstrokes, then use a lint-free cloth to wipe over the glaze. The color remains to highlight the detailing.

TIPS

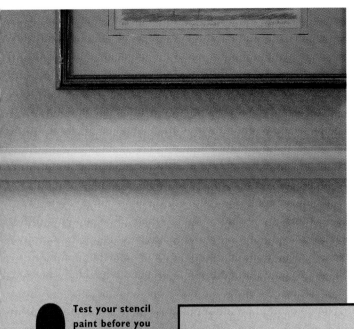

4 Stencil the cat

● Photocopy the stencil to your chosen size. Place the stencil so that the cat sits on the books; stencil in beige, gray, red and black, blending lightly.

5 Plan the mousehole

● With the compass point at floor level, draw a semicircle about 2" in diameter on the baseboard, about 6" away from the pile of books.

■ For any of these effects, if you do not have a picture rail, baseboard or chair rail, create one by masking off and painting a faux rail to give yourself an area to decorate.

■ To protect the paint on baseboards from wear and tear, apply at least one coat of clear varnish in oil- or water-based varieties, depending on the existing paint finish.

■ To add spot protection for stenciled designs, reposition the stencil exactly over the dry motif and spray with an appropriate varnish.

■ As an alternative to painting the eyes of the mouse, find a mouse motif that you can copy, color and cut out; then apply it as decoupage on the baseboard, just next to the mousehole.

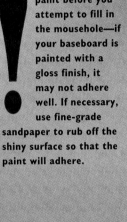

Test your stencil paint before you attempt to fill in the mousehole—if your baseboard is painted with a gloss finish, it may not adhere well. If necessary, use fine-grade sandpaper to rub off the shiny surface so that the paint will adhere.

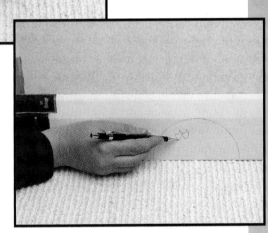

6 Add the mouse

● Using the pencil, draw in two eyes, looking upward toward the cat, in the top left-hand area of the mousehole.

7 Finishing touches

● Using the black stencil paint, fill in the area of the mousehole, leaving the whites of the mouse's eyes unpainted.

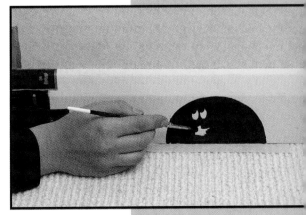

Freehand TECHNIQUES

Don't be daunted by the idea of freehand painting—it's simple to tackle if you plan carefully and take it in easy steps.

YOU WILL NEED:

- Flat latex paint in a variety of colors (red, pink, orange, blue, yellow, green, black and white)
- Medium-sized and small round artist's brushes
- Large, medium-sized and small flat artist's brushes
- Lining brush
- Small paintbrush
- Large paintbrush
- Permanent marking pens in purple and red-brown
- Varnish
- Mixing bowls
- Tape measure
- Ruler
- Pencil
- Circular item to draw around (such as a large bowl)
- Measuring cup
- Plastic plates or palette
- Cloths
- Stiff cardboard
- Scissors

Four-corner mural

This floral-design mural gives patterns and steps to a choice of motifs and borders—all you need is latex paint, artist's brushes and some simple planning.

From simple folk art to elaborate Eastern-style patterns, freehand painting is a colorful expression of individual style. It's all much easier than it looks, and you don't need any special artistic skills to create beautiful freehand designs. The important thing is to break the design down into simple steps. The finished motifs that make up this whole-wall design look complex but are surprisingly simple to create.

Basics and equipment

Choose your brushes carefully—they need to be soft-haired, such as imitation sable, in preference to hard-bristled ones, which will leave brushmarks. For sharp edges and straight lines, use a flat-tip brush with a squared-off tip. For circles, dots and other fluid brushstrokes, such as sunflower petals, use a round-tip artist's brush. If you intend to tackle a fairly large project, invest in several sizes of each brush type, including a lining brush.

Latex paint, when diluted slightly, is ideal for freehand painting. Use up leftover cans of paint or buy small cans, blending as you dilute the paint to make a wider range of colors.

Getting started

First of all, you need to plan the basic design on paper, starting with the four large floral patterns and adding the borders later so that you can be sure you have enough space left for the central motifs.

Before you start painting, roughly sketch each motif in pencil on the wall. This does not need to be perfectly accurate—it's just for use as a guide while you paint. Practice the brushstrokes on scrap paper until you feel confident controlling the brush and gauging how much paint to pick up on each type of brush.

Once you have finished painting, rub away any pencil marks, using a cloth moistened with paint thinner. In a kitchen or bathroom, or on surfaces likely to suffer wear and tear, protect the paint with a coat of varnish.

2 Paint two-color sunflower petals

● Load a medium-sized round artist's brush with yellow, then dip its tip in terra-cotta. Place the tip of the brush at the end of the petal, then press down the remainder of the bristles, dragging the brush up to complete the petal. Wipe the brush clean after each stroke, and reload with fresh paint.

1 Paint sunflower head

● Divide the wall area into four equal-sized sections, using the large bowl to draw a circle where the lines intersect. In the top left section, roughly sketch a sunflower, leaving about a 4"-6" gap between it and the pencil lines. Using a medium-sized round artist's brush and light dabbing strokes, fill in the center of the flower head with diluted terra-cotta latex paint.

Let paint dry at each stage before continuing—one hour should be enough. If you do not, the colors may bleed into each other, or you may smudge wet paint when you are working on another area.

3 Paint stem and leaves

● Using a flat artist's brush, fill in the stem with green latex paint. Then, before the paint dries, lightly paint a fine line of yellow latex paint along the top edge of the stem, blending it into the green. Repeat on the leaves.

4 Paint square motifs

● In the top right section, draw two squares overlapping at 45°, with a circle in the center. Divide the top square into four diamonds with spaces between them; using a flat artist's brush, paint each with deep pink latex paint, leaving the central circle unpainted.

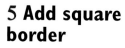

5 Add square border

● Using the lining brush loaded with blue latex paint, paint a fine line over the penciled outline of the second square, leaving a small gap unpainted where the pink squares overlap.

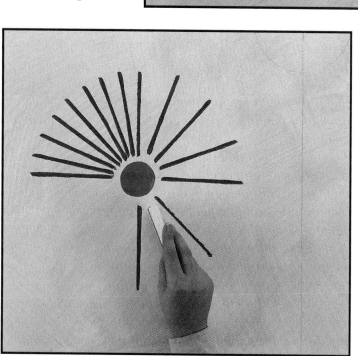

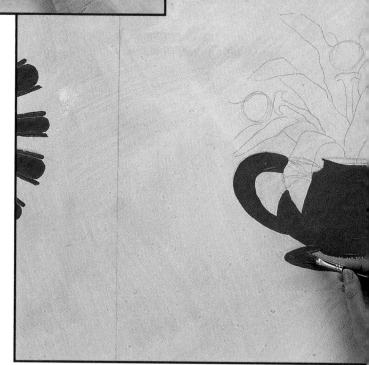

6 Add the daisy motif

● In the bottom left section, paint a small blue circle. Cut a 4"- to 6"-long strip of cardboard and load it with orange paint. Stamp the cardboard around the circle, starting with the four quarters, then filling in seven more petals between them. When dry, fill in alternate gaps between the orange lines to make blue petals.

7 Plan the tulips and the teapot

● In the bottom right section, roughly sketch the tulips and teapot. (Trace the design on page 46, if you want exact guidelines.) Using a flat artist's brush, fill in the shape of the pot with terra-cotta latex paint, leaving the areas where the leaves overlap the pot and the lip of the spout unpainted.

TIPS

■ Keep the base color on the wall pale, such as a gentle color wash that has only a slight variation in color and texture.

■ To create a gentle, chalky effect, wash over the finished design when it is completely dry with a thin white color wash, which will subtly tone down the colors.

■ For a more distressed-finish look, apply a thicker coat of color wash so that parts of the motifs are obscured. Lightly rub back other areas to produce a worn effect.

■ Remember, if your hand slips or if you make a mistake, you can always wait until the paint dries and neaten up the edges with a little of the background color.

■ When you are positioning the frame (step 10), do not leave too much unpainted space around the motifs, as this will produce a broken effect. But, on the other hand, do not cramp the motifs with a border that is too close. To get the right effect, try to allow roughly the same amount of space on all sides of the motifs.

■ Look to your own decorating scheme for inspiration for free-hand motifs or look at fabric samples, wallpaper, magazines and greeting cards.

■ Freehand painting is amazingly versatile. You can adapt the simplest design to suit the style of all types of decorating schemes, whether you decide to paint a large mural, add a colorful border around your walls or brighten up some accessories.

The stark, monochromatic design of the Japanese-style symbols, above, creates a dramatic focal point for a minimally decorated room. Cut several large sheets of textured paper into equal-sized rectangles, and with black India ink and a soft-bristled brush, paint random, abstract motifs and images. Attach the textured papers to the wall with wallpaper paste or ornamental tacks, or mount them in picture frames. Adapt the style of the motifs and the colors to suit your room—try using a scattering of small motifs over a whole wall to imitate designer wallpaper or use the same designs to accessorize smaller items in the room.

Different types of paint will create a variety of effects—artist's acrylic colors give a smooth, solid cover, whereas watercolors produce a soft, fluid and washy look, perfect for decorating or accessorizing a feminine bedroom or an elegant living room.

8 Paint tulip heads

● Hold the medium-sized flat artist's brush horizontally at the top left of the tulip head. Keeping a light pressure, pull the brush sideways to the right and then bring it around and down in an *S* shape, increasing the pressure until the bristles fan out and curve around, to complete one side of the tulip. Repeat in the reverse direction for the second side, adding an inverted *V* to complete the design.

9 Paint leaves green

● With a round artist's brush, fill in the leaves to complete the motif. To keep the leaves distinct and not appear as one green mass, leave small unpainted gaps where leaves overlap each other or bend over on themselves.

10 Draw a frame around motifs

● Leaving a 4"-6" gap around the motifs, frame them with a penciled rectangle. Add two penciled borders, 1½" and 4" respectively, outside this inner frame. With the large bowl, draw semicircles at the midpoints of the inner frame and quarter-circles at the corners.

11 Paint red and blue dots

● Using the round artist's brush, paint red circles 2"-4" apart along the frame and border around the motifs, making sure you start and end each line with a red circle. Then, using the small round artist's brush, paint a smaller blue circle between the red circles.

 You must start and end each line in the floral border with a red circle—the blue circle is too small to "hold" the design at the corners and edges, so any line that ends on a blue circle will look slightly short, spoiling the overall design. If you are unsure where to place the circles, mark the spacing with pencil marks before you start painting.

Design ideas

■ This elegant freehand border in rich gold liquid leaf over sumptuous red, left, makes a sophisticated decoration for furniture and accessories. It is made up of a combination of differently sized circles and lines, built up into a repeating border—this makes it easy to adapt to fit corners and unusual angles. Adjust the size of the circles and the spacing to suit the item you are decorating.

■ A simple stylized sunset, above, makes a border to brighten up walls, or if used as individual motifs, to decorate smaller items. Measure and mark the spacing with pencil marks, then add the sun in yellow. Draw the shapes of the sun's rays and reflection in pencil first, then paint over with a round artist's brush to avoid mistakes.

12 Finish the floral border

● Using the small round artist's brush, add purple pinpoint dots around the blue circles and short green strokes around the red ones. Paint a purple-and-green flower at the center, adding similar half and quarter flowers at the corners and midpoints.

13 Draw the spiral border

● Between the two outside pencil-line borders, use the purple marking pen to draw spirals roughly ¾" apart. Draw a half spiral at each corner, then add a line to separate the spirals, using the red-brown marking pen, and complete the border.

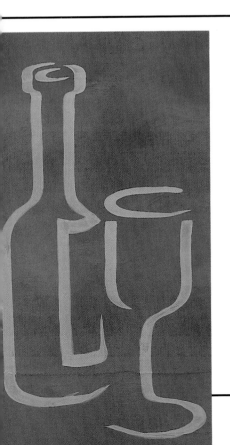

14 Add finishing line borders

● In the gap around the spiral border, add two more pencil-line borders. Paint the inner one with a lining brush and blue latex paint. For the outside border, pull the medium-sized round artist's brush along the pencil line, alternating the pressure on the bristles every ¾"–1¼" between light and heavy—this creates a beaded effect with a fine line when the pressure is light and a fanned-out shape when the pressure is heavier.

■ Once you have mastered the necessary brush control, there is no limit to the designs you can create, such as the classic, understated look of a simple line drawing as in the bottle and wine glass, left. To capture this look, draw the outline of your chosen item on paper, leaving gaps where the shadows fall. Test your design on paper until you are happy with its shape and proportion.

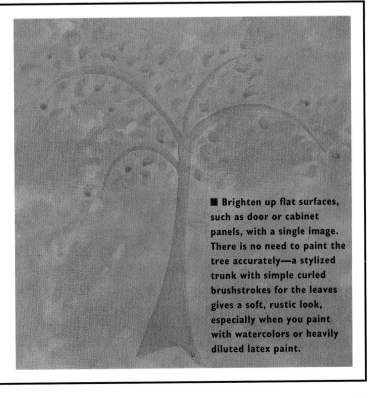

■ Brighten up flat surfaces, such as door or cabinet panels, with a single image. There is no need to paint the tree accurately—a stylized trunk with simple curled brushstrokes for the leaves gives a soft, rustic look, especially when you paint with watercolors or heavily diluted latex paint.

These **quick and easy** **techniques** are based on traditional stripes. **Create a** trellis pattern or stencil for a country look.

STRIPE
effects

This intricate-looking trellis pattern, opposite, is surprisingly simple to achieve. It's a clever variation on ordinary stripes, but there is no need for complicated measuring techniques. Just divide your wall into sections, using masking tape, and use this as the basis for your pattern.

1 Mask the stripes

● Over a base of lilac, start at the left end of one wall and use the plumb line and chalk to mark a 4"-wide vertical stripe. Leave a 2"-wide gap and draw in another stripe. Repeat, masking off the lines right across the wall.

2 Mark stripes

● Starting with the wide lilac stripe on the left, measure 4" from the top of the stripe and mark the inner edge of the tape on both sides. Measure 8" below these marks and mark again. Continue marking at alternating 4" and 8" intervals. Repeat on alternate wide lilac stripes. On the remaining stripes, make the first mark 6" from the top, then mark at alternating 4" and 8" intervals, as before.

3 Mask off the crosses

● Wherever a 4" interval is marked on the wide stripes, place masking tape to form a cross within the 4" space. The top edge of the tape at the top should abut the top marks and the lower edge of the tape at the bottom should abut the lower of the marks. Repeat over each 4" space.

YOU WILL NEED:
● 1½ quarts flat latex paint in lilac as a base (This may need two coats for good coverage.)
● 1 quart flat latex paint in pale pink
● 1 quart flat latex paint in pale gray
● Natural sponge
● Plumb line
● Chalk
● Masking tape
● Scissors
● Tape measure
● Metal ruler
● Pencil
● Craft knife
● Measuring cup
● Two saucers
The above quantities are sufficient to decorate a 12' x 15' room.

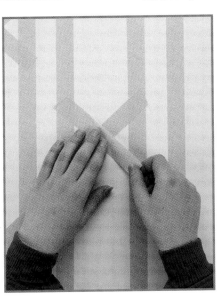

4 Trim around the crosses

● Using the craft knife and metal ruler, carefully trim away the masking tape from the vertical space between the arms of each cross, keeping the trimmed edge flush with the tape edge of the cross.

5 Sponge in two colors

● Pour some pink latex paint into a saucer and sponge lightly over the wall. Allow to dry, then sponge on the pale gray. Gently peel off the tape.

Stencil randomly over a background of pastel stripes for a pretty country look that is perfect for a dining room, bedroom or hallway. Choose small designs, such as flowers, leaves or cherries, so as not to overwhelm the stripe effect. Apply one (or, if necessary, two) coats of pink latex paint over the walls to provide a solid base color for this technique.

4 Stencil the leaves

● Mask off the leaf motif from the Flower posy stencil. Using the pink paint, sponge the stencil motifs randomly over the walls.

1 Plan the stripes

● Working from the left, measure and mark along the top of the wall at 4" and 2" intervals. Hang the plumb line from these points and make chalk marks down the string.

YOU WILL NEED:
● **Flower posy stencil from The Stencil Collection**
● **1½ quarts flat latex paint in pink**
● **1 quart flat latex paint in cream**
● **½ quart flat latex paint in terra-cotta**
● **2" paintbrush**
● **Household sponge**
● **Tape measure**
● **Chalk**
● **Plumb line**
● **Masking tape**
● **Scissors**

2 Mask off the stripes

● Apply masking tape to leave 4"-wide stripes fully exposed. The masking tape will almost fill the 2"-wide spaces.

5 Mask off again

● When the stenciling is completely dry, apply a second line of masking tape so that you leave a 3/16"-wide stripe on each side of the masked-off pink strips.

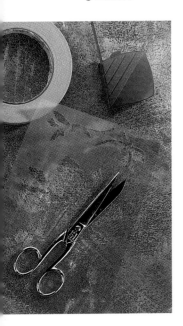

3 Paint the wide stripes

● Apply a coat of cream flat latex paint to the stripes and allow to dry for 2–4 hours.

! Make sure the stripes are dry before you start stenciling. If they are not, the wet paint will mix with the stenciling, making your motifs blurred and patchy.

6 Sponge on terra-cotta

● Pick up a little terra-cotta latex paint on a piece of sponge and dab over the thin stripes. Allow to dry for 2–4 hours, then gently peel away the masking tape.

Fantasy finishes

Inspired by nature—a starry, moonlit sky; the countryside in summer—these quick paint effects use sponging, color-washing and spattering techniques to transform walls with color and texture.

Starry sky bedroom

Create a dramatic midnight sky of deep blue and soft purple with clusters of stars, seen through wispy clouds and gently swirled by an invisible wind. This canopy of stars is the perfect finish for a romantic bedroom and is easy to produce with a combination of simple techniques that can be finished in a matter of hours.

Use diluted latex paint to give a quick-drying and translucent finish—by adding water you can make the paint go a lot further. The quantities given are sufficient to color-wash over the walls of a 12' x 15' room.

Variations

This paint recipe creates the effect of a midnight sky—but by varying the colors that you wash over the base of light blue, you can give the impression of a rosy, early evening sky, sponged in horizontal strokes, or an early morning light with washy layers of light grays and blues.

YOU WILL NEED:

- 2 quarts flat latex paint in pale blue
- ½ quart each flat latex paint in navy and purple
- 8 oz flat latex paint in white
- Large paintbrush
- Two bath sponges (see Tips, right)
- Denatured alcohol
- Measuring cup
- Three paint pails
- Cloths
- Scissors

1 Apply the base color

- Wash the walls with an all-purpose cleaner to remove any dirt or grease. When dry, apply an even, solid coat of pale blue flat latex paint. Allow to dry for 2–4 hours.

2 Apply navy patches

- Pour 5 parts navy latex paint into a paint pail, adding 1 part water to make a thick color wash. Using a sponge, rub the wash over the wall in short, circular strokes, creating random patches to cover half to two-thirds of the wall.

4 Rub back

● Dampen a cloth with denatured alcohol and rub over the wall, using random, circular strokes to blend and soften the texture of the color washes. In random areas, apply greater pressure to reveal some of the base color. Allow to dry overnight.

■ Bath sponges have a soft, open texture that is ideal for this technique. You can adapt an ordinary synthetic sponge by picking lumps out of it with scissors or your fingers.

■ If you rub the color back too much with the denatured alcohol, apply more of each wash, blending them into the overall finish. Once dry, gently rub back with a little denatured alcohol.

■ If you apply too much of the navy color wash and the whole effect looks too dark, rub back some of the heaviest patches heavily with denatured alcohol; apply extra purple wash over these areas, then rub back as before.

■ To increase the star effect, leave some areas of the white spattering unblended. To create a localized Milky Way, use a toothbrush to spatter up close in a swirled shape.

■ If the spattering dries before you have blended it, use some denatured alcohol to soften the texture.

5 Spatter with white wash

● In a pail, dilute some white latex paint with an equal amount of water. Pick up a little on the large paintbrush and standing 3' back from the wall, spatter randomly with a sharp, flicking action.

6 Blend the spattering

● While the white spattering is still wet, use a dry sponge in short, circular strokes to smudge and blend the white spattering gently into the background. Allow to dry for 1 hour.

3 Sponge on purple patches

● In a paint pail, dilute 5 parts purple latex paint with 1 part water. Using a clean sponge, apply over the wall using random, circular strokes, rubbing very lightly between the navy patches. Allow to dry.

! Spattering can be messy. Remove all furniture from the room and cover the floor, doors and any fixtures with drop cloths, taping them down firmly.

7 Spatter and blend navy

● Dilute the navy color wash with a little more water to get a thin consistency. Pick up a little on the paintbrush and spatter over the wall, then blend with a sponge as in step 6. Allow to dry for at least 3 hours.

Countryside view wall panels

Take a leaf out of the Impressionists' book to paint a vista of summery meadows, fading to a distant horizon under a twilight sky. The "window" panels, easily framed using decorative trim, make up for the lack of real windows in an inside bathroom, and you can adapt the colors of the view to be summery or autumnal or to give the impression of daylight.

The secret to this finish is a simple sponging technique—far easier than attempting to paint a realistic vista in all its detail. The effect is quick to complete too— each layer of water-based color dries in two to four hours.

Embellishments

Once you have mastered the technique, the concept is the same for creating a desert landscape, a garden with colored flowers or an alpine range—simply vary the colors and shapes. Increase the sense of perspective by adding a few hand-painted details, such as branches, flowers or foliage, in the foreground.

YOU WILL NEED:
- 8 oz flat latex paint in white, black, yellow, blue and several shades of green (or mix these shades with the blue and yellow)
- Large paintbrush
- Household sponge
- Decorative trim, sealed and primed with shellac, if new
- Tape measure
- Ruler
- Pencil
- Masking tape
- Scissors
- Paint pail
- Measuring cup
- Plastic plates
- Miter box
- Saw
- Finishing nails or nails appropriate to your surface
- Hammer

1 Base coat

● Measure and mark the position of the panels on the wall and mask off around the outside of each one. Paint the area inside the panels with mid-green flat latex paint, then allow to dry for 2–4 hours.

2 Texture the sponge

● Cut the sponge to roughly the size of your hand. Use a pair of scissors to trim off all the square edges; then pick random-sized lumps out of the flat surface with your fingers until the sponge has a honeycomb texture and soft, round shape without any hard edges.

3 Sponge on gray clouds

● Pour a little of each paint on a separate plate. Pick up a little white on the sponge, dab off the excess and starting at the top, sponge one-eighth of the panel in white. Blend black and white on a plate and sponge this into the white to create a mottled gray.

4 Sponge blues

● Pick up a little blue latex paint on the sponge and dab off the excess. Blend this into the bottom edge of the gray, slowly working in the color until no gray shows through the blue at the bottom edge. Sponge on the colors in a slight curve to give a greater feeling of perspective.

5 Blue shading

● Continue sponging with the blue paint until you are halfway down the panel, slowly increasing the intensity of the color by darkening the shade as you work downward.

6 Sponge and blend the greens

● Load the sponge with the darkest green, dab off the excess and start blending it into the blue. Sponge down the panel, gradually working each green in turn (getting progressively lighter) into the wet sponged edge until you have covered at least three-quarters of the panel.

7 Sponge yellow

● Pick up some yellow and blend into the lightest green, finishing the panel in pure yellow. As a final detail, lightly sponge a little yellow and lime green over the bottom quarter of the panel, barely blending them to create a sharper texture. Allow to completely dry.

8 Attach the trim

● Remove the masking tape. Cut the trim to size using the saw and miter box. Paint with white latex paint and when dry, nail in place.

! You need to work while the paints are wet for this effect to work. If the paint dries before you can blend it, you will have to wait for the edge to dry, repaint with the background color and start again when this is dry. Have the paints poured out and ready before you start and complete each panel in one session.

WAYS WITH DOORS

Add a touch of style to your doors. You'll be surprised by the effects you can achieve with paint, wallpaper and molding—and a few clever but simple techniques.

For all doors

● If a door is new, sand the surface with medium-, then fine-grade sandpaper, then apply a coat of primer. For a painted door, clean well with detergent or an all-purpose cleaner, fill any dents or cracks with wood filler and sand all over with fine-grade sandpaper. Wipe away all traces of dust with a damp cloth—and the door is ready to decorate.

YOU WILL NEED:
● Wood filler
● Putty knife
● Medium- and fine-grade sandpaper
● Cloth
● Water-based primer
● I quart satin-finish latex paint in base color
● ½ quart satin-finish latex paint in each of two colors
● I oz bottle water-based stencil paint
● Flower posy stencil
● 2" or 3" paintbrush
● 1½" paintbrush
● Measuring tape
● Chalk
● Long steel ruler
● Large set square
● Masking tape
● Scissors

Doors, when painted in plain, neutral tones, are often the dullest feature of any room—they are practical but uninspiring. Transforming a door is easy—effects with paint techniques are endless and can be combined with molding and decorative motifs to blend or contrast with your decor. As a caution, make sure you do not mix different types of paint—oil- and water-based, or flat, gloss and satin finishes; stick with one type and you can be assured of a good and lasting finish.

Preparing your door

Whatever finish you plan to give your door, you will need to prepare the surface, concealing any blemishes. For this you will need fine- and medium-grade sandpaper, a sanding block, all-purpose wood filler or wood putty, a putty knife, a soft cloth, primer and newspaper or a drop cloth.

Before you start, cover the surrounding floor with several sheets of newspaper or a large drop cloth, taping them in position, if necessary. Remove the door fixtures, then fill any cracks or holes in the door or door trim with wood filler, smoothing with sandpaper and a sanding block when dry. If you plan to paint the door, dust with a soft, barely damp cloth, let dry thoroughly, then apply primer to any areas where the paint is rubbed back to the wood. Allow to dry completely.

Faux painted panels

Bring a plain door to life with simple painted panels. The effect is quick and easy: Simply paint darker and lighter shades of the base color between strips of masking tape to create a trompe l'oeil molding effect. Add further interest with a stencil in one panel.

PHOTOGRAPHY BY LIZZIE ORME

1 Apply base color

● Paint the door with the base color, finishing ("laying off") the paint with vertical brushstrokes. Allow to dry (about 4 hours). Sand lightly with a fine-grade sandpaper to give a really smooth finish. Apply a second coat.

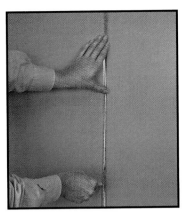

2 Mark the center

● With the door closed, measure from top to bottom and mark the halfway point. Mark lightly with a chalk line across the door.

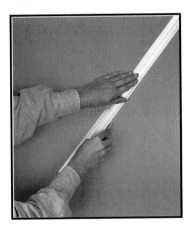

3 Mark centers

● Using a long ruler, draw crossing diagonals in chalk on both halves of the door. This marks the center points of the top and bottom sections.

4 Horizontals

● Mark points 5¼" down from the top of the door and 5¼" up from the centerline. Connect these horizontal lines, then repeat on the lower half of the door to mark the outer panel edges.

5 Verticals

● For perfectly right-angled corners, place the set square with its point at the intersection of the horizontal and the diagonal lines. Draw in the vertical lines on the top and bottom halves of the door.

6 Inside edges

● Tape a long ruler to the vertical line and place the set square on it, sliding it up so that the bottom edge sits 1¼" up from the bottom horizontal line. Repeat to mark the inner line on both halves of the door.

7 Masking tape

● Apply masking tape to run exactly down the outer edges of the panel lines to leave a 1¼" frame exposed for painting. Repeat on the lower half.

8 Paint the panels

● Mask off a mitered corner at the top right and bottom left corners of the panel to create a diagonal edge. Paint the top and left sides of the panels in the darker of your panel colors.

9 Second color

● When the first color is dry, reposition the corner masking tape to mask the other sides. Paint the remaining panel sides in the lighter paint; allow to dry.

10 Stenciling

● Mask off any flower stems on your stencil and form four flower motifs into a wreath. Stencil in the center of the panel, using water-based stencil paint.

1 Paint the door frame

● Clean, sand and wipe clean the door frame. Paint, using a color that matches the wallpaper and keeping the brushstrokes in line with the length of each side of the frame.

2 Mark the seam line

● Suspend a plumb line from the point above the top of the door frame where one strip of paper abuts the next. Mark the point with a soft-lead pencil and draw a vertical line as the join mark for hanging the paper.

EQUIPMENT

YOU WILL NEED:
● **Wallpaper to match the rest of your room**
● **Wallpaper paste**
● **Satin latex paint in same color as baseboard**
● **Satin latex paint in toning color for molding**
● **Trellis molding to fit door surround**
● **Architrave corner moldings**
● **Shellac**
● **Denatured alcohol**
● **2" paintbrush**
● **1" paintbrush**
● **Paste brush**
● **Smoothing brush**
● **Plumb line**
● **Soft-lead pencil**
● **Yardstick**
● **Long-bladed scissors**
● **White glue**
● **Papering table or long, flat work surface for pasting**

Make use of that extra roll of wallpaper and some simple molding to transform a door into an elegant feature of a room or hallway.

Wallpaper offers a variety of decorating opportunities—a plain door covered with the same paper as the rest of the room can look subtle and elegant. It can also create the illusion of space, making the room look larger than it really is, and it is the ideal treatment in, say, a hallway or landing where there are a lot of doors and doorways to distract the eye. This technique looks especially effective on plain cabinet doors.

Preparation

It is important to prepare the door for papering—a smooth surface is vital for a good finish. Any small speck of grit, which might not show on a painted surface, will become very evident if you paper over it, so check the door by feeling all over with your hand and sand it thoroughly. If there are any dents or cracks, fill these with all-purpose wood filler and when dry, sand down flush with the door. Sand all over with fine-grade sandpaper and wipe clean of dust with a damp cloth. To "size" the surface before papering, brush the surface with wallpaper paste to give a good "slip" to the wallpaper when you position it.

Matching patterns

Match the patterns of the paper on the door with that on the walls: Align the point where strips of paper join for a lateral match and line up the patterns across the strips for a vertical match.

3 Size the door

● Mix the wallpaper paste according to the maker's instructions, then "size" the door by brushing with paste. This gives good slippage when positioning the paper.

4 Match and cut the wallpaper

● Cut one end of a roll of wallpaper so that it matches the pattern above the door frame, allowing at least 3" above the top of the door itself. Measure and cut a strip of paper to match the height of the door, again allowing at least 3" extra at the bottom.

5 Paste the paper

● Lay the cut wallpaper on a papering table or long work surface and spread evenly with paste, making sure that you cover right to the edges.

6 Hanging paper

● With the door propped open, apply the pasted paper so that the pattern matches across the wall and door, and the vertical edge is flush with the pencil line. Working from the center out, smooth out air bubbles, using a smoothing brush. If necessary, lift and reapply for a smooth finish.

7 The second strip

● Cut the second strip to match the first, paste as before and apply by slipping the paper flat on the door until it abuts the previous sheet exactly and the pattern matches.

8 Prime the moldings

● If you are using plastic molding around the door frame, prepare the trim for painting by brushing all over with shellac, using a small brush. Make sure you work the shellac into all the corners, then allow to dry for about an hour. Clean the brush with denatured alcohol. To prime other surfaces, see Before You Paint, page 170.

9 Paint molding

● When the shellac is dry, paint the molding with satin latex paint in a color to coordinate with the wallpaper and contrast with the door frame. Allow 2–3 hours to dry, then apply a second coat. If you have corner molding, prime and paint in the same way, then place squarely over the corners of the door frame. Apply white glue thoroughly to the back of the painted molding and apply over the door frame (see Tips, right).

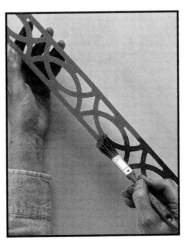

TIPS

■ To trim the top and bottom edges of wallpaper evenly, smooth the paper right to the top edge of the area you wish to cover, then fold or lightly score along the

line where you want to trim the paper. Fold the pasted paper right back from the top and cut along the marked line, then smooth the paper back into place with the brush. Repeat at the bottom edge.

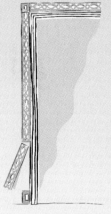

■ If moldings are not long enough to cover the sides of a door frame without a join, place the longer strip at the top and cut a smaller piece to fit the bottom where the join will be less obvious.

■ To carry pasted wallpaper, fold the top and bottom edges to the center, leaving about a 2" gap in the middle. Fold the unpasted side onto itself, then unfold, as necessary, as you hang it.

Add character and detail to plain doors with molding and decorative trim—they are inexpensive to buy and with a little careful measuring and positioning, they can produce a complete transformation.

By painting molding and other door trim, you can give an allover unified appearance—our plain door is decorated in a combination of cameo colors to give a classical look that coordinates with the elegant terra-cotta color-washing on the walls below the chair rail.

Preparing and planning

Careful measuring and planning is vital—it can make the difference between a symmetrical, polished result and an amateurish finish. If you find that your molding does not fit exactly into the diamond shape without cutting through the middle of one of the beads, follow the steps to adjust your spacing to get a symmetrical result. Remember, too, when you plan a feature such as a diamond shape on a door, that you must accommodate the door handle—so make sure that when reattached it will clear the molding by at least 1¼" to avoid making the door look cluttered.

Decoupage options

In place of ready-made motifs, you could use decoupage motifs. The advantage of these is that you can enlarge or reduce them to just the right size by photocopying—and the range of designs available in decoupage books is endless. Use diluted artist's acrylic colors to tint the motifs so that the original detailing shows through and position and apply them using white glue. Protect the finished door with two coats of flat varnish.

1 Paint the door

● Prepare and prime the door, then paint, finishing in even, downward strokes. Satin latex paint gives a slight sheen and, as it is washable, is more practical and durable than flat latex. It also dries faster and is easier to apply than oil-based equivalents. Allow to dry, then apply a second coat.

2 Measuring

● When the paint is dry, measure down the height of the door and mark the halfway point, using a piece of chalk or a soft-lead pencil. Repeat on the other side of the door. Measure across the top of the door and mark the center as before, then repeat across the bottom of the door.

YOU WILL NEED:
- ● Wood filler
- ● Putty knife
- ● Cloth
- ● Fine- and medium-grade sandpaper
- ● ½ quart primer
- ● ½ quart satin latex paint in cameo peach
- ● Wood bead molding, primed and painted in cream (see Help file)
- ● Button motifs or decoupage motifs
- ● Small and medium-sized paintbrushes
- ● Tape measure, ruler
- ● Plumb line
- ● Chalk or soft pencil
- ● Coping saw
- ● White glue
- ● Scissors

3 Mark the center lines

● Using a long ruler, connect the chalk marks to make a horizontal line across the center of the door. Do not press too hard when drawing the line, or it may be difficult to remove later. Repeat to mark the vertical center of the door.

5 Fit the molding

● To make a sharp point at the top and bottom of the diamond, saw two single beads from the painted molding. Apply glue to one bead and stick it on exactly over the marked top point. Position the second bead over the bottom point.

7 Adjust molding

● Hold the top right molding in position and mark where you need to cut it to fit perfectly. Cut and glue in position, then repeat with the other side to form a symmetrical shape.

4 Mark diamond

● Bearing in mind the position of your door handle, decide how close to the edges of the door you want the points of your diamond shape to be. Measure the same distance in from each side, then mark the top and bottom points at your chosen distance from the marked center points.

6 Cut the molding

● Measure the distance of one side and using the saw, cut two lengths of molding to fit the measured side (cutting one bead shorter rather than longer), and two strips a little longer than the measured side. Using white (carpenter's) glue, glue the top left and bottom right sides in place, tightly abutting the single top and bottom beads.

Finishing touches

Paint the door handle to match the molding and reattach to the door. To add extra decoration, paint small button or similar motifs in the same color as the cream molding and apply as directed below.

1 Apply paint

● Measure and mark positions in all four corners of the door that align with the points of the diamond shape. Do this by measuring in from the edges of the door, then check the accuracy of the positioning by holding up a long ruler or a flexible tape measure between the marks, making sure that they align with the points of the diamond.

2 Apply motifs

● Apply glue to the painted motifs and position carefully over the marked points.

PAINTED MOLDING

Although some molding is available ready to use in different colors of varnished natural wood, you need to prime unfinished molding before painting it. If you want to paint the molding with a satin finish to match the door, prime with a water-based primer, then apply two coats of cream satin latex paint to give a solid covering of color.

POSITIONING MOLDING

If you are not confident of getting your diamond shape perfectly symmetrical, use masking tape to position the strips of molding on the door so that you can adjust them to fit perfectly. Before using the masking tape, dab it across a piece of fabric to reduce the tackiness— this will prevent it from lifting off any of the base coat of paint when you remove the tape.

CORNER MOTIFS

Small button motifs can look too tiny on a large area such as a door. To make them larger, cut pieces of hardboard about ½" larger all around than the motif. Prime and paint these as for the motifs, then stick a motif onto the center of each one. Apply to the door as described on the left.

YOU WILL NEED:
- Wood filler
- Putty knife
- Cloth
- Medium- and fine-grade sandpaper
- All-purpose primer
- 1 quart satin oil-based paint in yellow
- Artist's oil colors in dark blue-gray and white
- 1 quart oil-based glaze
- ½ quart satin oil-based paint in both dull blue-gray and dull turquoise
- 2½" paintbrush
- Dragging brush
- ½" paintbrush
- Paint thinner
- Natural sponge

1 Color the glaze

● Squeeze a little artist's oil color in blue-gray and white into a small bowl and dilute with paint thinner. Stir well until the color has dissolved. Stir this into the oil-based glaze and keep adjusting the color with more diluted artist's oils until you create the color you want. If necessary, add paint thinner until the glaze is the consistency of thin cream.

P aneled doors offer an excellent opportunity to combine different paint effects and to color-coordinate your doors with the rest of the decor in a room. The mixed finish, left, uses a combination of oil-based primer, paints and glaze.

Prepare the door (see page 64), priming, if necessary, with an oil-based primer, then apply two coats of satin-finish (mid-sheen) oil-based paint in yellow (or your chosen background color) to the door frame, the baseboards and the door itself. Select a shade that either contrasts in tone with your intended dragging color or that is a complementary shade for the most effective results.

Mixing techniques

The paneled door is worked in a mixture of dragging and sponging—the door frame and the main stiles and rails of the door are dragged and the centers of the panels are sponged in two colors over the base.

Sponging in oil-based paint is just the same as for water-based paint, but you will need to use paint thinner instead of water to dilute the paint and to clean your sponge.

Order of work

Before you tackle the door, drag the door frame and the baseboards. Allow these to dry completely before you work on the door; otherwise, drag them when the door is painted. When dragging the door, follow the order of work exactly as detailed in each of the steps. Oil-based glaze dries to a durable finish, so there is no need to varnish the door.

2 Dragging

● Apply the glaze in even vertical strokes to the areas of the center stile between the panels and in horizontal strokes to the top, center and bottom rails. Dip the dragging brush in the glaze, squeeze off the excess, then drag the two areas of the center stile vertically, just overlapping the undragged glaze on the rails.

3 Drag the rails

● Wipe the dragging brush; then, starting from the top right corner of the door with the brush slightly overlapping the edge, drag straight across the top rail. Make sure as you cross the top of the center stile that you make a clean horizontal line at right angles to the center dragging. Repeat for the center and bottom rails.

4 Outer stiles

● While the glaze is still wet on the stiles, brush fresh glaze over the outer stiles, over the corners. Make sure you leave a clean edge of glaze in line with the side of the panel, at right angles to the dragging.

5 Drag the rails

● Starting at the very top of the door with the dragging brush slightly overlapping the edge, drag down the rails on both sides, making sure you leave clean lines where you cross the horizontal dragging.

6 First sponging

● Clean the edges of the dragging with a cloth dampened in paint thinner and allow to dry for up to 16 hours. When dry, blend a little of the dull blue-gray paint with half as much paint thinner or until it reaches the consistency of cream. Sponge lightly over the four plain panels. Allow to dry completely.

7 A second color

● Dilute the turquoise paint as in step 6 and sponge over the first layer, making sure you cover the whole area of the four panels. Allow to dry completely before painting the recessed surround on the panels.

8 Panel frames

● Using masking tape, mask off the areas on either side of the recessed surround on each door panel so that just the frame is visible. Using the small paintbrush, apply the dull blue-gray paint in horizontal strokes across the tops and bottoms and in vertical strokes down the sides. Allow to dry, then carefully peel away the masking tape.

Design ideas

Doors need never be boring—try some trompe l'oeil effects with stencils, highlight the doors as a special feature or blend them in with the surrounding wall—the possibilities are unlimited.

Midnight sky

▲ Paint the door in soft yellow, then when dry, glue on cutout star shapes at random intervals for a reverse stenciled effect (see Leaves on a Tray, page 129). Sponge in midnight blue, then when dry, remove the star cutouts.

Cottage door

◄ Paint the door in satin-finish oil-based paint in a honey color, then measure and mark a line across the door, just over half the way up the door. Mask off the area below the line and wood-grain over the top area. When dry, reposition the masking tape and wood-grain the lower area. Add a rustic stencil on the top section and either attach a latch, bolt and keyhole or paint these in, using artist's oil colors.

Bookshelves

Paint the door in dark blue, then paint the ▲ frame and "shelves" in a color to match the baseboard. Cut several different book-spine shapes out of stencil acetate and use these to fill the shelves, with some books standing and some at an angle or horizontal.

Soft sponging

▲ If you have sponged walls and want to make your room as spacious as possible, blend the door with the surrounding areas by sponging it in the same colors. Use a toning color for the baseboard and frame to make them less conspicuous.

Garden room

◄ Make a door look like the entrance to an arbor of flowers by stenciling an arch shape in crisscross trellis in water-based paint. When this is dry, stencil a tangle of climbing roses over the top.

CHAPTER 2

Special Effects with Paint

Leather effect

Give plain furniture an opulent finish with stylish faux leather. Using ordinary oil-based paint and artist's oil colors, the effect is surprisingly easy to achieve.

Leather desktop

Embossed leather, with its distinctive texture and rich colors, has been used for centuries as a traditional inlay for desks or panels or for upholstering furniture. Authentic embossed leather has a rich, opulent quality and is expensive—however, there is a simple faux technique that can add the same touch of elegance at a fraction of the cost.

This simple technique lends itself well to trompe l'oeil inlays and even a faux upholstered look, complete with buttons and brass upholstery tacks.

The drawer of the leather inlaid desk (opposite) is, in fact, completely false—a faux leather panel has been added to a fake drawer front with a brass handle to add the finishing touch.

Because the effect is worked in artist's oil colors and oil-based paint, it does take a while to dry between coats, especially as the layers are applied quite thickly. Make sure one coat is completely dry before you start the next stage of the technique.

YOU WILL NEED:

- Oil-based primer
- 1 quart oil-based paint in white
- Artist's oil color in crimson lake
- Paint thinner
- Gold liquid leaf
- Oil-based matte varnish
- Medium-sized and small paintbrushes
- Lining brush
- Masking tape
- Scissors
- Medium-grade sandpaper
- Lint-free cloths
- Mixing bowl
- Household sponge

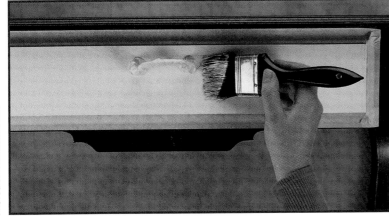

1 Sand and prime the surface

● On the desktop, measure a rectangle the same width as the drawer and 4" in from the front and back edges, then mask off. Mask off the drawer front, covering the decorative edging. Sand the masked-off areas, prime and allow to dry. Apply an even coat of white paint and allow to dry.

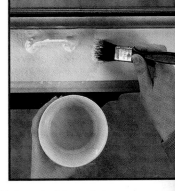

2 Apply and stipple tinted paint

● Pour some white oil-based paint into a bowl and tint with a little crimson lake oil color to make a soft pink. Apply a thick coat of the paint inside the masked-off panels, then stipple with the medium-sized brush to create a rough texture. Allow to dry overnight.

3 Rub on the oil color

● Dampen a cloth with paint thinner, load with a little crimson lake oil color and rub over the surface in circular strokes. Allow to dry 30 minutes.

4 Skim off some of the color

● Using the flat edge of the household sponge, lightly skim over the crimson lake oil color to remove some of the color. Allow to dry overnight.

5 Paint on gold lines

● Remove the masking tape. Using the lining brush and gold liquid leaf, carefully paint around the edge of each panel. Varnish when dry.

WALLPAPER AND FABRICS FROM ARTHUR SANDERSON & SONS LTD. GREEN CHAIR FROM GEORGE SMITH

YOU WILL NEED:

- Oil-based primer
- I quart oil-based paint in white
- Artist's oil color in terre verte and black
- Oil-based matte varnish
- Paint thinner
- Small and medium-sized paintbrushes
- Upholstery tacks
- Ruler
- Pencil
- Masking tape
- Flexible masking tape
- Scissors
- Medium-grade sandpaper
- Lint-free cloths
- Two mixing bowls
- Household sponge
- Awl
- Hammer

EQUIPMENT

Leather fire screen

Stylish, deep-buttoned leather upholstery adds a touch of luxury to any home, but the genuine article can be expensive. Using the faux leather paint effect and a clever but simple trompe l'oeil highlighting technique, you can add your own tufted-leather look to small items of furniture, such as this fire screen, or give an opulent coordinated look to a set of chairs with plain wooden backs.

You don't need any special skills to copy the three-dimensional tufted-leather look—you create highlights around each button by simply wiping away paint around one side and adding a shadow on the opposite side to balance the effect. A mix of terre verte and black oil colors produces a soft green, but traditional browns, reds and burgundies—or even fantasy colors—will look just as effective.

77

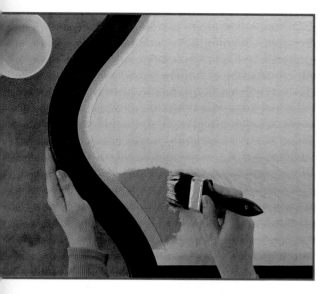

1 Stipple tinted oil-based paint

● Measure and mark a border around the fire-screen that is 3" deep at the top and bottom and 2" wide on each side; mask along the outside, using flexible tape for the curve. Sand the surface; apply a coat of primer and then white paint, drying between coats. Apply a thick layer of white paint tinted with terre verte, stippling to give a textured effect. Allow to dry overnight.

2 Plan and mark buttons

● Working on a diagonal, measure and mark the positions of the buttons, spacing them 4"–6" apart. Draw a small circle around each pencil mark as an outline for the button.

Color guide

■ You don't have to limit yourself to traditional browns or dark reds for your faux leather—this striking rich blue effect was created using French ultramarine artist's oil color rubbed on a stippled base of white oil paint tinted with the same shade.

■ For a dramatic purple faux leather effect, use Winsor violet artist's oil color over a stippled base of white oil paint tinted with the same shade. To make a darker purple, add a touch of burnt umber to the paint.

3 Paint the buttons

● Dab a little tinted paint over the pencil marks inside the circles. After several hours, press each painted button with your fingertip to make a hollow imprint. Allow to dry completely.

4 Apply oil color

● Using a cloth damped with paint thinner, rub some terre verte oil color over the surface. Let dry for 30 minutes, then using the sponge, skim over the terre verte to remove some of the color. Allow to dry overnight.

5 Add the highlights

● With a piece of cloth wrapped over your finger, wipe off some of the oil color in a semicircle around the right side of each button. Then wipe the left side of the button itself to reveal the base color.

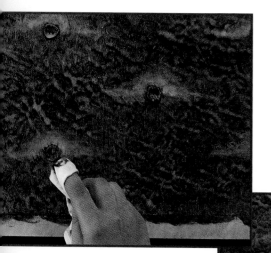

7 Add finishing touches

● Apply at least one coat of varnish and allow to dry for 12–14 hours, then remove the masking tape. Make pencil marks at 1" intervals around the edge of the leathered area. Using the awl, make an indent at each mark, then hammer the tacks into the holes.

6 Add shadows

● In a bowl, mix black and terre verte oil colors and pick up a little on a clean cloth. Apply gently in a semicircle around the left side of each button. Apply a little oil color to the right side of the button itself. Allow to dry overnight.

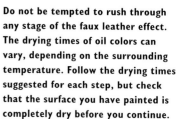

Do not be tempted to rush through any stage of the faux leather effect. The drying times of oil colors can vary, depending on the surrounding temperature. Follow the drying times suggested for each step, but check that the surface you have painted is completely dry before you continue.

Leather binders

Before

Using this faux paint technique, you can transform ordinary office-style binders into stylish leather-bound books, fit to grace the grandest library shelves. Follow the steps for the leather "inlaid" desktop on page 75 but use raw sienna mixed with a little burnt umber instead of crimson lake. The gold lines and marks along the spine of each binder, which emulate the elaborate gold lettering of expensive leather-bound books, are easy to create. Use a little gold liquid leaf to paint on a simple impression of one or two lines of text—there's no need to paint the actual characters. Paint the lines on the spine by eye, but if you don't feel confident about working freehand, lightly draw in some soft pencil guidelines to follow, taking care not to score the surface.

To give a three-dimensional effect, pick up a little burnt umber oil color on an artist's brush and add a shadow beneath each gold line. When the oil color is completely dry, apply one or two coats of oil-based gloss varnish to protect the finish, allowing to dry completely between coats.

Floating MARBLE

This is the simplest of fake marble effects—and it is perfect for any horizontal surface. The texture has the same speckles and veins as real marble, but there are no set shades to match and no limits to the colors you can use.

YOU WILL NEED:

- 1 quart oil-based paint in white
- Artist's oil colors in white, orange, red and yellow shades
- 1 quart paint thinner
- 1 quart oil-based glaze
- Medium-sized paintbrush
- Large, soft-bristled fitch
- Softening brush
- Round badger brush
- Small firm-bristled brush
- Paper towels
- Cheesecloth

The above quantities are sufficient to give a floating marble finish to the side and end panels of a tub surround and to coordinate bathroom cabinet panels, as well.

Just as in the true marbling technique, floating marble uses a base of oil-based paint with a blending of colors of oil-based glaze over the top. This forms the base of the effect—then a spattering of paint thinner over the surface breaks up the colors and eats into the glaze to create veins, rings and patches.

Materials and colors

The technique itself is simple, but you do need some specialty equipment, which cannot be improvised. The two main brushes you need are a thick round fitch—a

The very pronounced speckling on the right was created by blending glaze in light yellow and green with highlights added in rusty brown-tinted paint thinner. The wetter the glaze and the more paint thinner you spatter over it, the more exaggerated the marbled effect will be.

1 Preparation

● Paint the panels with white oil-based paint and allow to dry for up to 16 hours. Squeeze a little of the oil colors for the main color into a small bowl and add a little paint thinner. Mix well to dissolve the paint and adjust the color. Remember that when mixed with the glaze, the paint color will become much lighter. Pour about 12 oz of glaze into a bowl and stir in most of the colored mixture. The consistency should be like thin cream. Reserve a little and set aside. Repeat with the second, darker color of glaze.

PHOTOGRAPHY BY LYNDON

2 Apply glaze

● With the tub panel lying flat, pick up some of the main background glaze on the soft fitch and spread it randomly all over the painted surface, crisscrossing the strokes and leaving uneven patches of color, almost as if applying a coat of color wash.

START AGAIN
Because the whole effect is created in wet oil-based glaze, it is easy to wipe the background clean and start again if you make a mistake or do not like the way colors look together. Dampen a lint-free cloth with paint thinner and use it to clean away the glaze while it is still tacky.

SPOT REPAIRS
If there is just a small area that does not look quite right, dampen the bristles of a soft fitch with paint thinner and lightly brush over the problem area. Start again from the beginning with a little more colored glaze.

COLORS
To alter the color balance of a piece of floating marble, adjust the intensity of the color of the tinted paint thinner. When you are ready to stipple over the marbling with the soft badger brush, you can make the overall appearance slightly lighter or quite noticeably darker by adjusting the color of the glaze before you stipple it on.

soft, round-shaped bristle brush—and a badger brush. The latter brush is important because the bristles form round spikes when dampened with paint thinner, and this is essential for the broken marbled effect. But you can substitute a toothbrush for the firm fitch used for spattering and you can use a soft shaving brush in place of a more costly softening brush.

You can use any combination of colors you like. Practice blending colors of oil-based glaze and see the effects produced by different intensities of color. Because glaze is translucent, you need a very deep color for a dark background.

Surfaces

For floating marble, you need to work on a flat, horizontal surface, so remove cabinet doors or panels before you marble them. This is because the technique relies on spattered droplets of paint thinner standing on the surface, and if this is tilted, the paint thinner will run and create dribbles. Otherwise, any smooth surface to which you can give an oil-based painted finish is suitable for floating marble.

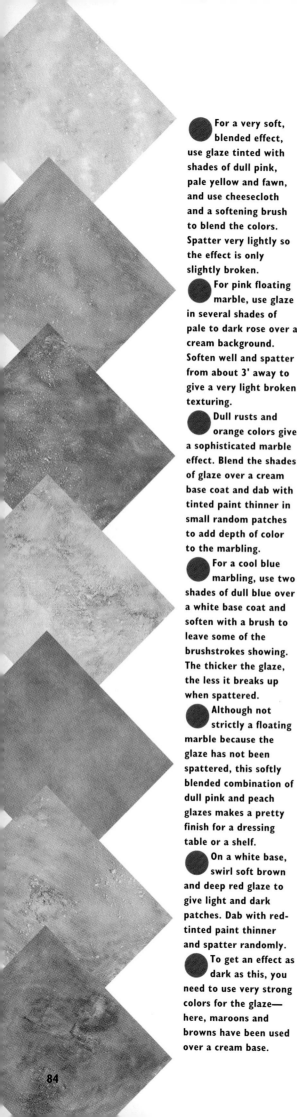

● For a very soft, blended effect, use glaze tinted with shades of dull pink, pale yellow and fawn, and use cheesecloth and a softening brush to blend the colors. Spatter very lightly so the effect is only slightly broken.

● For pink floating marble, use glaze in several shades of pale to dark rose over a cream background. Soften well and spatter from about 3' away to give a very light broken texturing.

● Dull rusts and orange colors give a sophisticated marble effect. Blend the shades of glaze over a cream base coat and dab with tinted paint thinner in small random patches to add depth of color to the marbling.

● For a cool blue marbling, use two shades of dull blue over a white base coat and soften with a brush to leave some of the brushstrokes showing. The thicker the glaze, the less it breaks up when spattered.

● Although not strictly a floating marble because the glaze has not been spattered, this softly blended combination of dull pink and peach glazes makes a pretty finish for a dressing table or a shelf.

● On a white base, swirl soft brown and deep red glaze to give light and dark patches. Dab with red-tinted paint thinner and spatter randomly.

● To get an effect as dark as this, you need to use very strong colors for the glaze—here, maroons and browns have been used over a cream base.

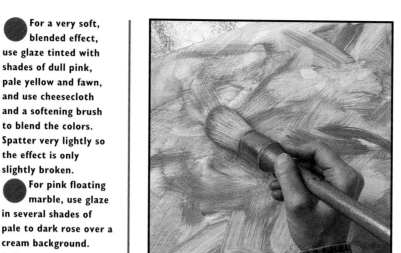

3 Glaze highlights

● Wipe the fitch clean on paper towels; while the first color of glaze is still wet, brush the second color over the top, this time spreading it on in random streaks to give an uneven patchy appearance. This will create a shaded effect when the two colors are softened together.

4 Soften the glaze

● For a very soft effect, dab the still-wet glaze lightly all over with cheesecloth to break up the brushstrokes. To break up the effect further, use a softening brush to blur the edges. Flick the brush lightly over the glaze so that the two colors blend smoothly into each other.

● If you want the lines in the painted glaze to be more pronounced, do not use the cheesecloth to soften the brushstrokes and use only the brush to blend together the edges of the different colors. Whichever way you choose, the effect will be broken up when you add the paint thinner.

TIPS

■ Remember that unless you use very pale and subtle colors, the effect of floating marble can be quite striking, so it is best to use it as a decoration for relatively small areas, such as panels, shelves or tabletops.

■ Floating marble takes up to 24 hours to dry; since it is hard to remove dust or pet hairs without spoiling the effect, allow to dry in a closed room.

5 The speckled effect

● Dip a soft badger brush into paint thinner, wipe off the excess on paper towels and stipple it randomly over the colored glaze. The hairs will clump together in small round spikes, and as you dab these over the glaze, the paint thinner breaks up to form rings and speckles.

● Using the same brush, dip the tips of the bristles lightly into the leftover colored paint thinner and dab over the surface to give an uneven blotching of color. The additional paint thinner will break up the surface even further. Repeat this process in different patches using the second color of paint thinner. If you like, adjust the colors to add extra shading.

■ This tabletop was marbled with glaze tinted with deep kingfisher, lighter blue and sandy yellow oil colors, which when blended create blue-green shading. By spattering only lightly, you get a soft, less defined speckled effect.

6 Spattering

● While the whole surface is still wet, dip a firm-bristled fitch into paint thinner; steadying the head of the brush with your thumb, use your index finger to spatter paint thinner over the glaze. For a very pronounced effect, flick quite hard so that the drops of paint thinner splash quite fiercely into the wet glaze.

7 Finishing touches

● If the effect is not pronounced enough, use the firm fitch to stipple paint thinner over the surface. When complete, allow to dry in a horizontal position, taking care not to disturb the wet glaze when you move it.

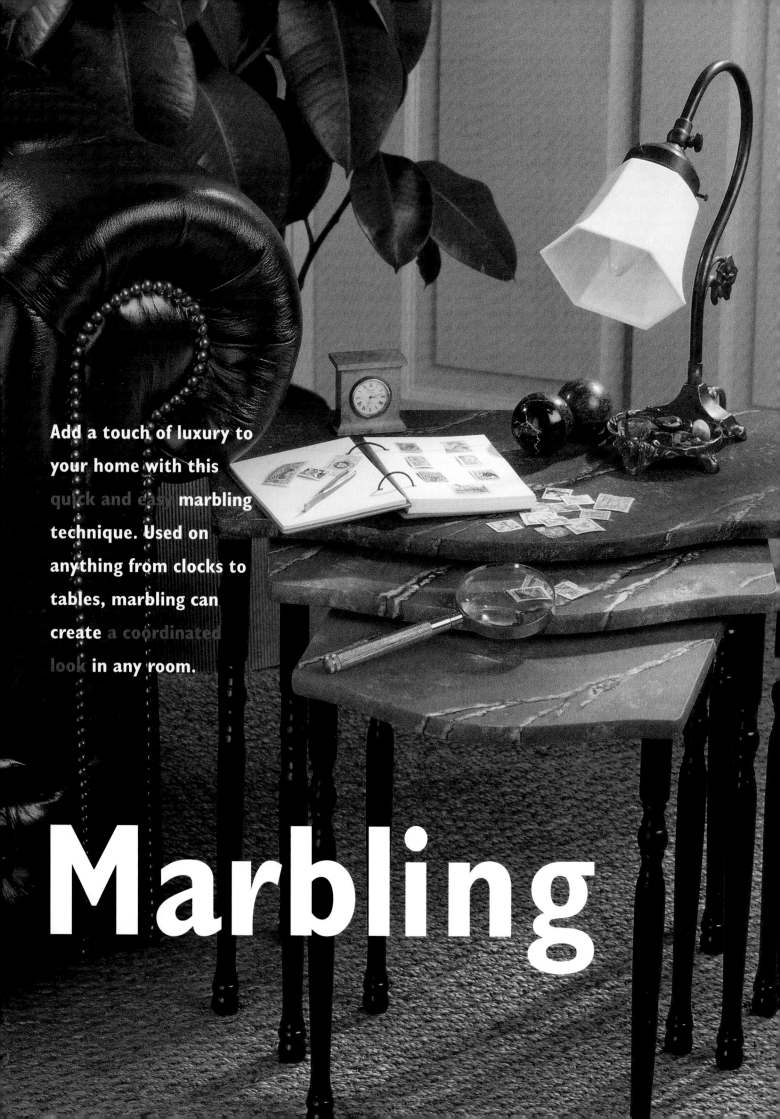

Add a touch of luxury to your home with this quick and easy marbling technique. Used on anything from clocks to tables, marbling can create a coordinated look in any room.

Marbling

PHOTOGRAPHY BY ADRIAN TAYLOR

EQUIPMENT

YOU WILL NEED:
- White oil-based paint
- Artist's oil colors in yellow ocher and raw sienna
- Paint thinner
- High gloss varnish
- Two medium-sized paintbrushes
- #10 artist's brush
- Round-tip fitch
- Sword striper
- Fine artist's brush
- Household scouring sponge
- Black wax crayon
- Medium- and fine-grade sandpaper
- Lint-free cloths
- Three paint bowls
- Plastic spoons
- Craft knife

Faux marble dates back hundreds of years and owes its evolution to the high cost and limitations of the genuine article. Ceilings and beams were marbled, as the stone was too heavy to use in these places, while imitation marble fireplaces and furniture were cheaper than the real thing. Traditional marbling methods, however, could be complicated and often needed great skill to perfect. This up-to-date technique is easy to follow and uses only simple materials.

The technique

Over a smooth base of oil-based paint, apply two glazes made simply by mixing artist's oil colors with paint thinner. Unlike traditional marbling, you do not add the colors to an oil-based glaze. Blur the surface with a brush, mottle with paint thinner and draw in the veins with a sword striper. Add detail with a wax crayon—a lot easier than using a fine brush or feather, the traditional way—then soften the veins with an artist's brush.

1 Preparation

- Sand down the surface with medium-grade sandpaper and wipe clean, using a cloth dampened with paint thinner. You will need two coats of oil-based paint to give a smooth surface. Apply the first coat and allow to dry for up to 16 hours. Sand with fine-grade sandpaper before applying a second coat. Wipe again with a cloth dampened with paint thinner to remove all traces of grease.

2 Make up the glaze mixtures

- To make up the glaze mixtures, squeeze a little yellow ocher and raw sienna into separate bowls and add paint thinner; mix well to dissolve the paint. The consistency of each glaze mixture should be like a thick syrup.

3 Apply the glaze

- Apply patches of yellow ocher glaze mixture all over the surface with the #10 artist's brush. Work diagonally across the surface. Fill in the gaps with raw sienna, again using the #10 artist's brush. As the glaze is thick, use sparingly.

SEA GRASS FLOORING FROM CRUCIAL TRADING LTD.

Color guide

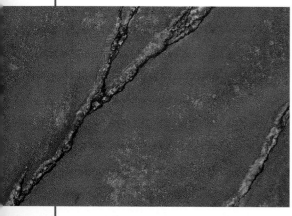

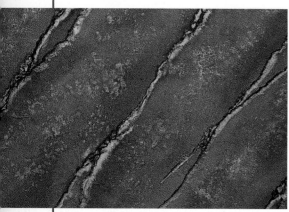

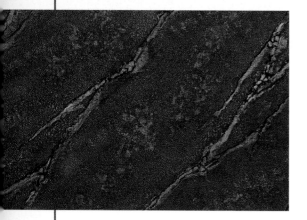

Marble comes in a wide variety of colors. For the steps, we imitated Sienna marble (as on the small table, pictured on page 86), which you can vary endlessly. For the mid-sized table, we created a pinker Sienna marble, using raw sienna and flesh tint along with a black wax crayon for veins. Make sure you use less than half as much flesh tint as raw sienna, or the finish will be much too pink. For the large table, we made up a rich brown version with raw sienna and burnt sienna, again using a black wax crayon to create the veins.

4 Blur the edges

● Blur the edges between the two colors and any brushmarks, using the round-tip fitch. Use the fitch in a gentle vertical dabbing motion, keeping up a very light pressure. Try to work over an area only once; if you do too much, the color variation will disappear.

5 Soften the glaze

● Pour some paint thinner into a bowl. Cut a small square from the household scouring sponge, using the craft knife, and dampen with paint thinner. Dab the sponge side of the scourer randomly over the surface. The paint thinner will mottle the oil glazes to create a feeling of depth. Paint thinner spreads quickly, so err on the side of caution until you see how the mottling progresses.

6 Paint the veins

● Load the sword striper with paint thinner and paint on a few veins (too many will spoil the effect). Let the sword striper wobble as you draw it through the oil colors. Allow the veins to "open" for 15 minutes before continuing.

HELP FILE

■ As a guide, veins should be at least 8" apart. Draw them roughly in the same direction—on the diagonal, never horizontal. Connect some veins or taper them away at different angles to give a natural look.

7 Draw along the veins

● Using the wax crayon, draw along one edge of each vein. Always stick to the same side of the veins (here, the left-hand side). Again, let the crayon wobble as you draw. When you come to the end of a vein, do not draw a solid line, but draw several small dots, instead. Blur with an artist's brush (step 9) to merge the dots to form a thin, tapering line.

8 Draw in the pebbles

● Where the veins join, you will find patches of pale glaze mixture, as the paint thinner will have dispersed most of the color. You can disguise these pale areas by drawing in several small circles to represent pebbles, which are characteristic of this type of marble. Again, wobble your hand as you draw in the pebbles to give a natural effect.

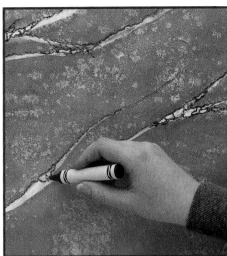

9 Finishing touches

● Now gently blur the veins with a fine, dry artist's brush. Work your way along each vein, with the brush perpendicular to the direction of the vein. In a light seesaw motion, dab the surface to blur the wax crayon line. Vary the degree of blurring, so the finished effect is not too uniform. When the surface is completely dry (let dry for at least 48 hours), coat with a high gloss varnish. Apply at least two coats, leaving the first to dry before applying the second.

SEAN ELLIS

Before

Marbled clock

Marbling works equally well on smaller items, which you can use to complement marbled furniture or walls, creating a luxurious, coordinated look. For our striking black-and-gold marble clock, we used ivory black mixed with burnt umber to create a single glaze mixture, drawing the veins with a gold wax crayon. You could use a second glaze in dark brown or gray. Soften the glaze thoroughly or the black background can appear flat.

TIPS

■ The final color will be determined by how much of each glaze mixture you use. If you are unsure, apply equal amounts of both. Remember, dark colors stand out more than light, so if you want the colors to appear in even proportions, apply less of the dark color.

■ To get rid of scratches in the marbling, apply a tiny amount of undiluted oil color to the surface. With a small, dry artist's brush, stipple the affected area until the color blends in. For smaller damage, use a tiny amount of glaze and again stipple the surface with an artist's brush. For vein damage, dab the affected area with the crayon and blur.

■ Before you varnish, the surface must be completely dry. If it is not, the paint will lift. If possible, leave the finished item for several days in a warm place (a heated room is ideal).

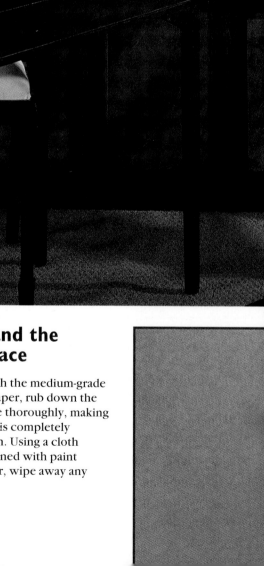

EQUIPMENT

YOU WILL NEED:

- ● I quart oil-based paint in white
- ● Artist's oil colors in ivory black, madder brown and raw sienna
- ● Paint thinner
- ● I quart oil-based gloss varnish
- ● Two medium-sized paintbrushes
- ● Household sponge
- ● Feather
- ● Medium-grade sandpaper
- ● Lint-free cloths
- ● Large mixing bowl
- ● Three small mixing bowls
- ● Mixing sticks

This second marbling technique is more traditional than the first but the idea is the same. The effect reached a peak of popularity with the Victorians, who used it on every conceivable surface, often decorating places where it would have been impossible or impractical to use real marble. Just as there are infinite variations of the stone in nature, so it is possible to achieve a wide variety of faux marble finishes. Choose a color to suit your decor, from gray to ocher or sage green. For the markings, you can use bold, striking patterns of veins, such as those in the first technique, or opt for a subtler effect. In this second marbling feature, the technique is more traditional and the look is softer—delicate patterns of fine veins are painted over a background of cloudy, blended shades of brown. These markings make it perfect for large areas such as paneling, doors or woodwork, while you can still use it to coordinate smaller items of furniture and accessories.

The technique

The basic technique is simple—mix artist's oil colors with paint thinner and use this to make up two differently colored glaze mixtures. Apply the glaze mixtures to a surface previously painted with oil-based paint, soften and blur them, then etch in a tracing of veins. This time, in contrast to the first marbling technique, the colors are blended and softened much more and the veins are drawn in with a feather. Experiment with a feather to see the effects it creates—the look varies from fine single lines to thicker, fractured veins made up of a tracery of tiny, threadlike lines.

1 Sand the surface

● With the medium-grade sandpaper, rub down the surface thoroughly, making sure it is completely smooth. Using a cloth dampened with paint thinner, wipe away any dust.

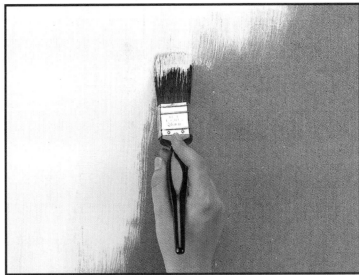

2 Apply the base coat

● Pour some white oil-based paint into the large mixing bowl and add a little ivory black artist's oil color. Stir thoroughly until the paint turns a pale gray. Using a medium-sized paintbrush, apply an even coat over the surface to be marbled; let dry for 12–14 hours.

3 Make the glaze mixtures

● To make the glaze mixtures, squeeze a little madder brown and raw sienna artist's oil colors into separate mixing bowls and dilute with paint thinner. Mix well until each mixture has a thick, syrupy consistency.

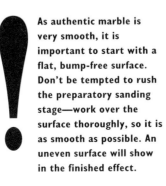

As authentic marble is very smooth, it is important to start with a flat, bump-free surface. Don't be tempted to rush the preparatory sanding stage—work over the surface thoroughly, so it is as smooth as possible. An uneven surface will show in the finished effect.

4 Apply the first glaze mixture

● With a medium-sized paintbrush, apply the madder brown glaze mixture in random diagonal patches across the surface.

5 Apply the second glaze

● With a medium-sized paintbrush, apply the raw sienna glaze to the surface, filling in the gaps between the madder brown. Apply the glaze with light, horizontal, crisscross brushstrokes, working down each section.

6 Blend the glaze

● Tear or cut the household sponge in half, using one piece dry to soften and blend the wet glaze patches.

7 Soften the glaze

● Dampen the other half of the sponge with paint thinner. Dab it randomly over the surface until the glaze mixture starts to lift off slightly, creating a mottled effect.

Color guide

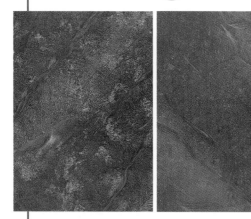

These different marble finishes were both created using the same colors and materials. For the marbling on the right, the veins were placed where the two glazes meet, emphasizing the color difference. For a dramatic finish, add veins that contrast completely with the background glaze. The marbling on the left, on the other hand, has veins that run randomly across each color band, and more paint thinner was used to soften the surface (see step 7), so patches of base color show through to give a mottled finish.

8 Make the black glaze mixture

● In a bowl, mix a little oil-based paint and paint thinner with ivory black artist's oil color. Dip the feather into the mixture, gently wiping off the excess on the side of the bowl.

9 Draw in the fine veins

● To draw plain fine veins, hold the feather with the quill side nearest to you so only the very edge touches the surface. Drag it lightly along, working in a diagonal direction. Let your hand wobble so the line is not perfect.

10 Draw fractured veins

● To create fractured veins, start as in step 9 and in one continuous movement flatten the feather against the surface, drag in a sideways action and bring it back to its original position.

11 Apply varnish

● When you have finished adding the veins, allow to dry for at least 48 hours before coating with gloss varnish. Apply at least two coats, making sure the first is completely dry before you apply the second.

Design ideas

Subtle, feather-veined marbling works well on small and large items alike. To create a coordinated look, use it on accessories such as this cheese board, which started out as plain wood. For the cool, gray marbling, use a base coat of white oil-based paint and a single glaze mixture, made up of titanium white with a touch of ivory black. Add veins in sage green. If you are marbling surfaces that will take a lot of wear and tear or that will come into contact with food, it is important to apply several coats of the appropriate varnish.

As real marble occurs in an infinite variety of shades and patterns, you can choose virtually any colors for your faux marble. Here, a plain trinket box was transformed with elegant lilac marbling. The base color is lilac oil-based paint, with a single glaze of Prussian blue over the top. The delicate pattern of veins is in viridian. If you are marbling a small, curved item, take care when adding the veins. Practice before you start, as dragging the feather across a curved rather than a flat surface takes a lighter touch.

TIPS

■ If the glaze dries too quickly, you will find it difficult to soften and blend, so wipe it off the surface with a cloth dampened with paint thinner and start again. Add a little more artist's oil color to each glaze mixture, as this will slow down the drying process. It is a good idea to test your glaze mixtures on a small patch of the surface you are going to marble.

■ Before you start drawing in the veins, practice on a scrap of cardboard. Use the feather to try out the techniques for creating fine and broken veins. If the surface you are marbling is relatively small, you could even draw a pattern of veins to use as a guide later on.

■ Don't be tempted to add too many veins to your marbled surface, as this will make the finished effect look cluttered. Draw them roughly in the same direction, running diagonally, not horizontally, across the surface. Also, make sure that none of the veins cross each other.

Malachite

You need only the simplest of materials—and a deceptively simple technique—to recreate the whorls and patterns of this richly colored green mineral.

YOU WILL NEED:

- Dark-tinted oil-based gloss varnish
- White oil-based paint
- Gold metal paint
- Artist's oil color in viridian
- Oil-based gloss varnish
- Paint thinner
- Medium-sized and large paintbrushes
- Small, coarse-bristled artist's brush
- Medium- and fine-grade sandpaper
- Lint-free cloth
- Masking tape
- Scissors
- Mixing bowl
- Mixing stick
- Cardboard (see Tips)

Based on the beautiful patterns of malachite, this simple paint technique captures the rich, deep tones of the green mineral. Although the real stone is usually found only in small quantities, this faux effect can be used over larger areas to give a look of luxury to furniture or on door panels, as shown opposite, just as well as for highlighting accessories or smaller items.

To make the finished effect look as realistic as possible, study authentic examples of malachite, looking especially at the pattern and shape of the crystal formations.

The technique

Unlike many traditional faux paint effects, this technique uses no specialty brushes or equipment. The most important consideration is the surface, which must be smooth and, if possible, flat so that the whorls of the pattern flow evenly. Sand the surface thoroughly, then, over a base of emerald green, stipple on viridian artist's oil color, using a paintbrush. The distinctive patterns found in malachite are easy to reproduce with a piece of torn cardboard. A defining line around the whorls and some smaller circles complete the effect. When dry, add a coat of gloss varnish to give it a protective finish and the characteristic shine of the polished stone.

PHOTOGRAPHY BY ADRIAN TAYLOR

95

1 Prepare the surface

● Remove any hinges and door fixtures from the door. Sand the surface first with medium- and then with fine-grade sandpaper until the wood is clean and smooth. Dampen a cloth with paint thinner and wipe away any dust or grease from the surface.

2 Stain the bare wood

● Bare wood is easily marked by accidental splashes, so you need to varnish around the panels before you start the malachite technique. Mask off the inside of the panels and coat the rest of the door with the dark-tinted varnish. Remove the tape and allow to dry for 12–14 hours.

3 Paint the base color

● Reposition the tape to mask off around the outside of the panels. Pour some white oil-based paint into a mixing bowl and tint with a little viridian oil color. Coat each panel with the tinted paint and allow to dry for up to 14 hours. If this looks patchy, apply a second layer, sanding lightly between layers.

4 Tear the cardboard

● Tear thick cardboard into 4" strips. Fold these strips every 2 ½"–3" and tear apart at the folds. Do not cut the cardboard with scissors, as this will give a smooth finish—the edges need to be slightly rough to create the right effect.

5 Stipple top color

● Dab some undiluted viridian oil color on the panel in random dots, using a paintbrush. Swirl the bristles of a large paintbrush over the dots of oil color to distribute it over the surface, then stipple the oil color with the same brush to give a mottled texture and to remove any brushstrokes.

6 Create the malachite patterns

● Applying firm pressure, drag the torn edge of the cardboard through the wet artist's oil color in circles that randomly and occasionally overlap. Keep one side of the cardboard roughly in the center of the circle and wobble the cardboard to give the characteristic uneven edges of the malachite whorls. Use a cloth to wipe excess color from the cardboard and replace it with a fresh piece when it becomes saturated.

7 Outline the whorls

● Drag the handle end of the artist's brush through the wet color about ¼"–½" from the outside edge of each whorl to give an outline.

8 Add small whorls

● In the center of every whorl, twist the artist's brush in a tight circle to cover any slip marks made by the edge of the cardboard. Add small whorls by repeating the twisting action randomly over the surface, breaking up large whorls and filling any plain areas. Remove the tape and let dry in a well-ventilated room for at least 48 hours.

9 Paint a gold border

● Mask on both sides of the recess around the panel; using the medium-sized paintbrush, apply a coat of gold metallic paint. Remove the masking tape and allow to dry for at least 12 hours.

10 Varnish the door

● Mask off around the entire panel, then apply an even coat of oil-based varnish inside the masking tape. Remove the masking tape and allow to dry for up to 14 hours. To enrich the color of the wood stain on the rest of the door, mask off the panels and apply a second layer of dark-tinted gloss varnish.

Malachite is ideal for transforming small accessories. Prepare porous surfaces with oil-based primer and use small pieces of cardboard to create the whorls on small or curved areas. Protect the newly painted surface with gloss varnish.

TIPS

■ Cardboard from breakfast cereal boxes is ideal for this technique. This cheap-quality cardboard gives a slightly uneven edge when it is torn, making a perfect patterning tool. Above all, never use corrugated cardboard.

■ Hold the cardboard in any way that is comfortable, as long as you keep it fairly rigid and maintain a smooth, even pressure on the surface.

■ Because you cannot turn your wrist in a full circle, you will need to reposition your fingers when drawing a complete whorl. Do not lift the cardboard from the surface, as this will create a broken effect.

■ Instead of tinting oil-based paint with artist's oil color, you can use ready-mixed emerald green, but be careful—colors vary a lot between different brands.

Tortoiseshell

Capture the beautiful, translucent reddish-brown tones of tortoiseshell
with this easy-to-master faux paint effect. Using simple and inexpensive materials,
bring an exotic touch to furniture and accessories.

YOU WILL NEED:

- White oil-based paint
- Artist's oil colors in yellow, raw sienna, burnt umber and burnt sienna
- Paint thinner
- Oil-based satin varnish
- Medium-sized paintbrush
- Softening brush
- Three small or medium-sized stencil brushes
- Masking tape
- Scissors
- Medium-grade sandpaper
- Lint-free cloths
- Two mixing bowls
- Mixing sticks
- Plastic plates or palette

aux tortoiseshelling has been used for centuries to recreate the deep, mottled texture of a sea turtle's shell. The technique was originally developed in the 17th century to compete with imports from the Far East. This up-to-date method uses inexpensive materials and needs no special skills to bring an exotic touch to your home.

Tortoiseshell, imitation or real, was most often found as an inlay or overlay detail on furniture or on small items, such as picture and mirror frames. Victorians extended the paint effect to cornices, ceilings and woodwork. Today it is one of the most versatile faux effects—suitable for furniture, accessories and even walls.

Blending the colors

For a realistic effect, the colors need to be accurate. For the perfect tone, paint patches in raw sienna, burnt umber, and burnt umber and burnt sienna mixed together. Be cautious—too much burnt sienna makes the finish too hot, and too much burnt umber makes it too dark.

Before

1 Sand the surface

- Mask off the trunk's metal trimmings. Sand the wooden areas with medium-grade sandpaper until the surface is smooth so that the base color will adhere. Dampen a cloth with paint thinner and wipe away any traces of grease and dust from the surface.

2 Apply the base color

- In a bowl, tint the white oil-based paint with a little yellow artist's oil color. Apply an even layer to the wooden areas of the trunk and allow to dry for 12–14 hours. If necessary, apply a second coat to get an even and solid base.

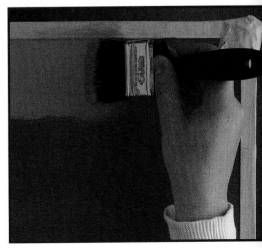

99

3 Apply the first color

● Squeeze some raw sienna artist's oil color onto a plastic plate and load a stencil brush with the paint. Working diagonally from top right to bottom left, dab the oil color on the surface in a zigzag pattern to form patches that are 2 ½"–4" long and about the same distance apart.

4 Apply the second color

● On the plate, mix burnt umber with three times as much burnt sienna. Take a clean brush and keeping to the same diagonal, apply between the raw sienna in patches that are slightly smaller than those in step 3.

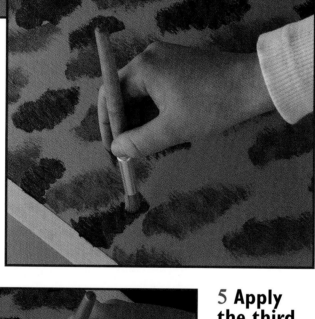

5 Apply the third color

● Squeeze some burnt umber onto the plastic plate and apply in patches that are at least half the size of the other colors; err on the side of caution as too much burnt umber will spoil the effect. Do not fill in all the gaps between the different patches; a little of the yellow base should still show through.

Color guide

Following the same technique, create a stunning red tortoiseshell. Tint white oil-based paint with scarlet lake to get a dusty pink for the base. Apply large diagonal patches of scarlet lake and smaller patches of burnt umber. After softening, spatter with black.

Create a stylish finish, using the colors of nature. Tint white oil-based paint with sap green for the base layer. Apply diagonal patches of sap green and burnt umber, using more of the green—too much burnt umber will muddy the effect. Soften and then spatter with burnt umber.

Mix yellow ocher with white oil-based paint for the base color. Apply diagonal patches of burnt sienna and yellow ocher, using more of the latter to lighten the overall effect. Soften, spatter with burnt umber glaze and soften again for a strong, rich variation to blonde tortoiseshell.

A deep blue fantasy finish is perfect for a bathroom. Over a base of white oil-based paint tinted with coeruleum blue, apply patches of Prussian blue and coeruleum. For a light and sparkling finish, apply larger patches of coeruleum. Soften and spatter with a raw umber glaze.

6 Blend the colors together

● While the oil colors are wet and still working on the diagonal, work the softening brush in light, sweeping strokes over the surface. Continue until the patches blend together, leaving no distinct edges.

9 Soften the spattering

● Working in the same diagonal direction as before, flick the softening brush over the surface, using very light strokes. Only soften across the surface twice, otherwise the spattering will disappear. Allow to dry for 24–48 hours.

7 Mix the glaze

● Squeeze some burnt umber artist's oil color into a bowl and mix with a little paint thinner, stirring well until the color is evenly distributed and you have a fairly thick but free-flowing syrup. Only mix up a small amount—the glaze will be used for spattering, and a little will cover a large area.

8 Spatter with glaze mixture

● Load a stencil brush with the burnt umber glaze and spatter over the whole surface by tapping the brush against a brush handle. Make sure all areas are lightly and evenly covered.

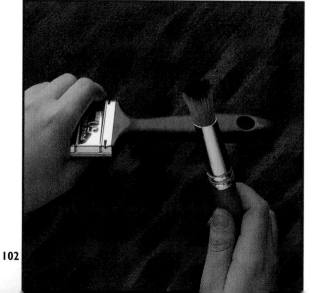

10 Apply the varnish

● Once the surface is completely dry, apply at least one coat of oil-based satin varnish. Allow 12–14 hours for each coat to dry before removing the masking tape.

Design ideas

ELIZABETH WHITING ASSOCIATES

HELP FILE

■ The color and markings of real tortoiseshell vary from one piece to the next, so if you want a realistic finish, look at a few examples before starting your project.

■ Adjust the size and shape of the artist's oil color patches according to the size of the surface you are working on.

■ If you are unsure which shade to tint the white oil-based paint with, choose the artist's oil color that you will use the most of to complete the effect. Or use the paint untinted, making sure no white shows through in the finished effect.

Traditionally, tortoiseshell is used in small quantities, but with this paint effect, it is easy to transform large, plain objects, such as the tabletop, above. Use patches of artist's oil color in keeping with the table's proportions and coat with exterior varnish to provide lasting protection.

Smaller accessories, such as this smart trinket box, make perfect quick projects. Create natural tortoiseshell for an understated effect or try a fantasy finish in shades that match your decor. For an ornate look, decorate with a black, silver or gold trim.

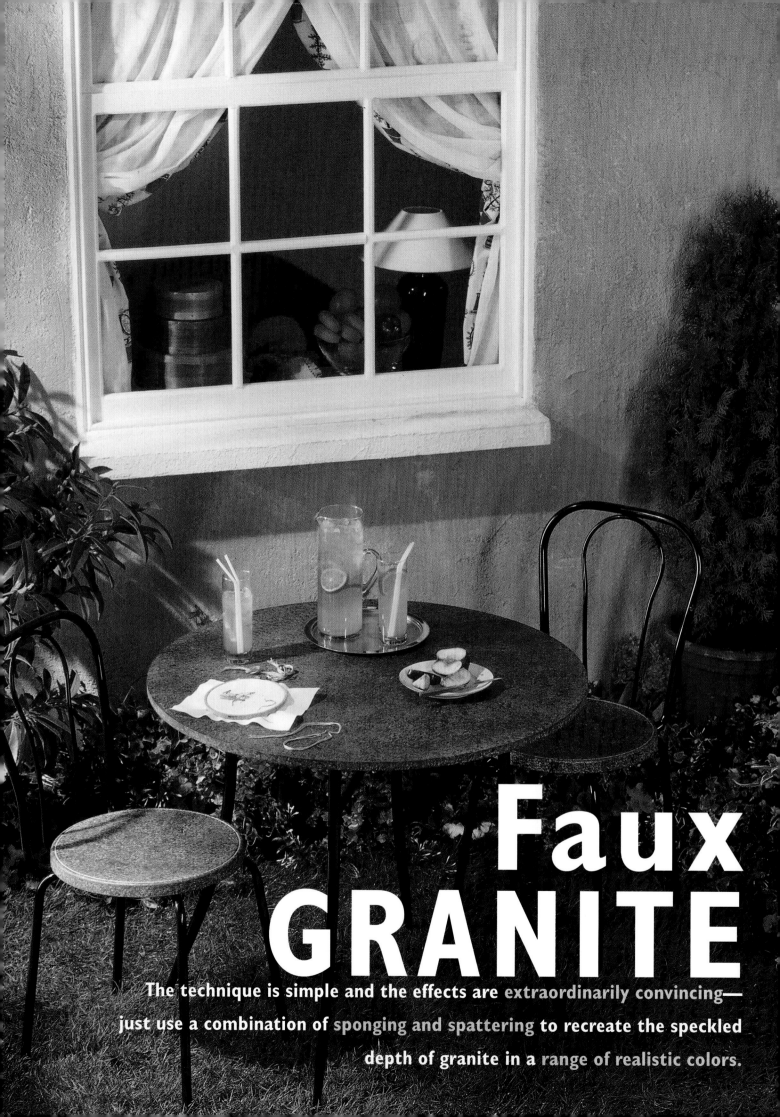

Faux
GRANITE

The technique is simple and the effects are extraordinarily convincing—
just use a combination of sponging and spattering to recreate the speckled

depth of granite in a range of realistic colors.

Garden furniture

There is no mystique to this simple faux effect—it is easy to create by building up a textured depth of color in tones that imitate the look of real granite.

Suitable surfaces

Granite is an ideal treatment to lend weight to inexpensive garden furniture, revamp ordinary pottery and vases or add a touch of class to accessories, such as a lamp base. Choose items that normally might be made of granite; you are unlikely to find whole walls in granite, but panels or pillars would look convincing.

The surface needs to be primed properly to ensure that the finished item will stand up to wear and tear, but it does not have to be completely smooth. For instance, you could use the technique on particleboard, but you would need to take care that the texture does not make the sponging look blotchy.

PHOTOGRAPHY BY ADRIAN TAYLOR

YOU WILL NEED:

- ½ quart red oxide metal primer
- I quart flat latex paint in ivory
- Small cans flat latex paint in brown, black, dark gray and mid-gray
- Matte acrylic varnish
- Three small paintbrushes
- Household sponge
- Two sea sponges
- Manicure brush
- Coarse- and medium-grade sandpaper
- Lint-free cloth
- Drop cloth
- Four plastic plates
- Plastic spoons for mixing
- Construction paper
- Paper towels
  The above quantities are sufficient for a table and four garden chairs.

1 Prepare the surface

- Sand the surface thoroughly with coarse-grade sand-paper, then finish with fine-grade sand-paper so the paint will adhere well. Wipe with a damp cloth to remove the dust.

2 Apply the primer

- Brush an even coat of red oxide primer over all the areas to be textured. This is very difficult to remove from clothes, shoes or floors, so work on a drop cloth and wear protective clothing as you work. Allow to dry completely—this will take about 24 hours.

3 Apply the base color

- Apply a first coat of ivory flat latex paint and allow to dry—this will take 2-4 hours, depending on the temperature. Apply a second coat of ivory paint.

4 Even the texture

- While the second coat of paint is still wet, dab lightly all over with the sponge to even out the brushstrokes. This gives the effect a more realistic finish.

TIPS

- To create a realistic mottled effect when sponging, use different areas of the sponge and vary the pressure you use for each color according to which shade you wish to show the most.

- If you find that one color seems over-dominant in the sponging, work over the area again in another color to balance the effect.

- Avoid spattering overlarge dots on top of the sponging. It is better to use very little paint on the brush and build up the color in a greater number of small dots than to spatter too heavily.

- Granite is a natural igneous rock formation and often has traces of silvery mica in it. Imitate this by using silver metallic paint in place of one of the sponged colors—or create a different look with bronze metallic paint instead of brown.

105

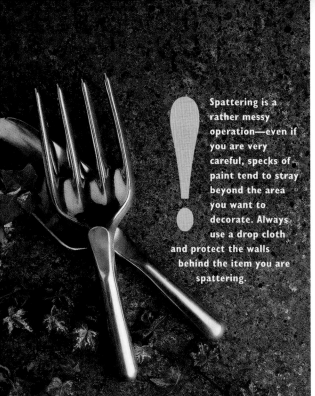

8 Damp sponging

● While the brown sponging is still wet, use a slightly damp sea sponge to soften the effect. Allow to dry for up to 1 hour.

9 Layers of color

● Repeat steps 6, 7 and 8 with the dark gray, mid-gray and black, as shown above. Build up the layers of color gradually, softening and drying between colors. Do not use too damp a sponge for softening, or the mottling will become blurred, and make sure that the sponging is still damp when you dab over it with the dampened sponge.

5 Prepare the paint

● Pour a little brown, black, gray and mid-gray latex paint onto separate plates; stir in a little water to dilute the consistency so that it is slightly thicker than that of thin cream.

6 Dab off the excess

● Check the texture of the paint—if it is too runny, it will form splotches. Load a sea sponge with the brown paint and dab off excess onto construction paper.

10 Spattering

● Place the item you are painting on top of a drop cloth. Using the diluted black, load a manicure brush with color.

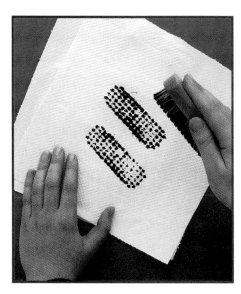

7 Sponge the first color

● Sponge the brown paint lightly over the ivory base to create a soft dappling of color. Wash the sponge in warm water immediately after use.

11 Remove excess paint

● Dab off excess paint from the manicure brush onto paper towels. Although it will take longer to cover the area, this is an important step, as an overloaded brush will create large, ugly blobs of paint; the ideal appearance is a very light, even dotting.

12 Spatter the surface

● Hold the manicure brush with the bristles uppermost and angled slightly toward the sponged surface. Draw your fingers through the bristles to create a light spotting. Reload the manicure brush as necessary.

13 Protect with varnish

● When the spattering is dry (about 1 hour), apply at least two coats of matte varnish, drying between coats. For extra protection against wear and tear, apply a third coat.

◀ Apply decorative moldings with glue before painting in ivory. Sponge over the top in brown, gray, silver and pale green, then add a light spattering of black.

Design ideas

Use different color combinations to give the appearance of different types of granite. The effect is perfect for urn-style vases, goblets or accessories, and provides a quick face-lift for all manner of junk-shop finds.

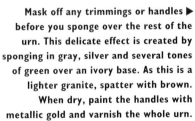

◀ Starting with an ivory base, this vase is sponged in two shades of red, brown, gold and dark gray. A spattering of black adds the final touch to give a feeling of depth to the finished item.

Mask off any trimmings or handles ▶ before you sponge over the rest of the urn. This delicate effect is created by sponging in gray, silver and several tones of green over an ivory base. As this is a lighter granite, spatter with brown. When dry, paint the handles with metallic gold and varnish the whole urn.

Moiré

Bring the luxury of moiré silk to your home with this easy-to-master paint technique. Subtle tones work together to give a delicate and sophisticated finish to any room.

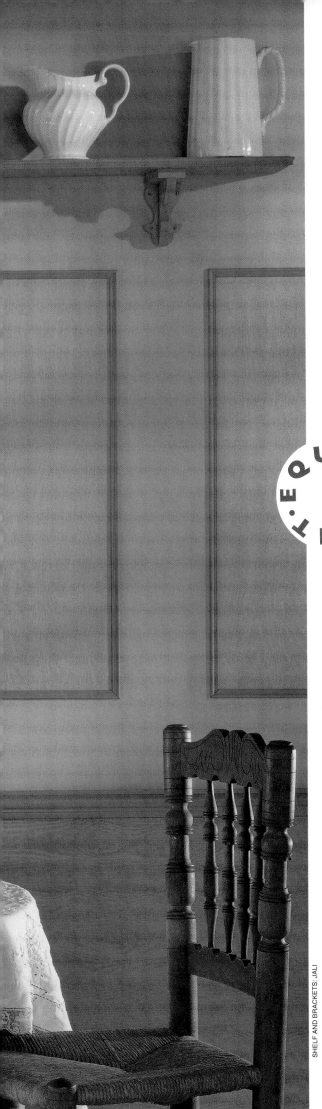

SHELF AND BRACKETS: JALI

PHOTOGRAPHY BY MARK WOOD

E·QUIPMENT·

YOU WILL NEED:

- 2 ½ quarts of flat latex paint in light green and dark green
- Water-based acrylic transparent glaze
- 1 quart of flat latex paint in mid-green
- Two medium-sized paintbrushes
- Small paintbrush
- Softening brush
- Rocker-type wood-graining tool
- Masking tape
- Scissors
- Measuring tape
- Chalk
- Ruler
- Plumb line
- Plain white paper
- Paint pail
- Mixing sticks
- Lint-free cloths
- Molding
- Pencil
- Saw
- Tack hammer
- Finishing nails

The quantities given are sufficient for a 12' x 15' room.

Moiré silk is a fine, luxurious watermarked fabric—its subtle tones and fine texture work together to produce a delightfully delicate pattern. Typically, moiré is used in small, defined areas, such as panels on walls or doors; it was once fashionable to line the panels of wardrobe doors with silk. It is, however, quite expensive and as a wall covering can be impractical, as it needs custom cleaning. Instead of using the fabric, you can imitate its subtle tone-on-tone pattern and texture using a process similar to basic wood-graining.

You do not need special skills or equipment and you can use the technique on any flat surface—as long as it is smooth enough for the wood-graining tool to go over.

The Technique

After applying a thin layer of tinted water-based acrylic glaze over a flat latex base coat, the wood-graining tool is used to create a grain running vertically down the wall. The texture is softened, first with the combing edge of the graining tool, and then with a softening brush. For the wall, the process is repeated, but this time the grain is drawn in a horizontal direction. As the water-based glaze mixture dries quickly, it is best to progress in sections, working nonstop from the wood-graining through to the softening.

Materials

Unlike wood-graining, the moiré paint effect uses tones of the same color for the base and glaze mixture. If there is too much of a contrast, the finished effect can look crude. It is a good idea to test the colors you have chosen before you start, as they can look quite different together when they dry.

1 Paint the wall

● Prepare the wall: Wipe down to remove dirt; prime, if necessary. Mask off the chair rail and paint the wall above with the light green latex paint. Then apply a coat of dark green latex paint to the wall below the chair rail. Allow to dry for 2–4 hours.

4 Draw in vertical lines

● Hang the plumb line so that it intersects the marks made in step 3. Chalk down the plumb line at regular intervals until you reach the lower guide. These marks will complete the outlines for your panels. Use a set square to check that each corner is a perfect right angle. You can also use a spirit level to check your horizontal lines.

If you add too much latex paint to the glaze, it will drastically reduce the drying time. This will make the glaze mixture extremely difficult to work with.

2 Draw the panel guides

● Using the chalk and tape measure, mark a point 6" down from the top of the wall, and 6" up from the chair rail. Repeat these chalk marks at regular intervals along the wall. Now, using the ruler, connect the dots to make two straight lines.

5 Mask off the guides

● Now mask around the outside of the guides. For added protection from paint splashes, you can cover the gaps in between each panel with plain paper and hold in place with masking tape.

3 Mark panel widths

● Find the wall's center point; mark 12" on either side along each chalk line. This will give you guides for a 24"-wide panel. Allow a 6" space on each side, then mark two 12" panel widths. Continue to mark panel guides in alternating 24" and 12" widths along the wall.

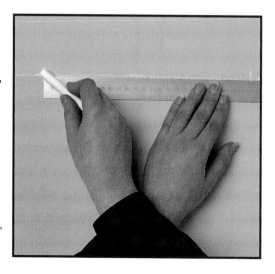

6 Mix the glaze

● Pour some of the acrylic glaze into the paint pail, and add a little mid-green flat latex paint. Stir well until the color is evenly distributed. You only need a small amount of flat latex paint to color the glaze.

7 Apply the glaze

● With a medium-sized paintbrush, working in vertical strokes, apply a thin layer of glaze to the panel. Work in strips about 20" wide so that the glaze does not get a chance to dry before you have finished.

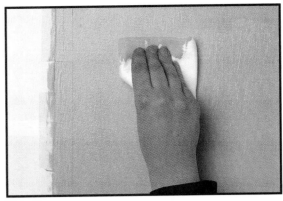

8 Dab off excess glaze

● As soon as you have applied the glaze, take the lint-free cloth and very lightly dab some off, so that more of the base color shows through. Make sure you do not remove too much.

9 Wood-grain vertically

● Wood-grain in vertical stripes down the glaze, overlapping each band slightly. Work several hearts into the grain at different heights—do not use too many, or the pattern will be too busy. Every so often, wipe the tool clean with a cloth, as it will not work properly if it is clogged up.

10 Comb the grain

● To soften and add texture to the grain, turn the wood-graining tool around and using the comb edge, run down each band. Work quickly, as you will not be able to comb effectively if the glaze begins to dry.

■ Whatever design you choose, a plan will help you visualize the finished effect. Make a plan of your design on paper before you start. It is best to work the panels from the center point of a wall, to give symmetry to the design.

■ Do not worry if the combing is not quite straight. The technique is looser than wood-graining, so straight graining is not as important.

■ If you can, get someone to help you. As the glaze dries fairly quickly, it is easier if one person paints it on while the other grains and combs.

11 Soften the glaze

● When the glaze has just started to dry, soften the surface with the brush, using vertical and horizontal strokes. This imitates the crosswise grain of moiré.

12 Cut the molding

● Measure all the molding to fit your panels, then cut the molding to size, using the saw and miter box.

13 Paint the molding

● With the small paintbrush, apply an even layer of the dark green flat latex paint to the molding. It is much easier to paint the molding now, before you attach it to the wall.

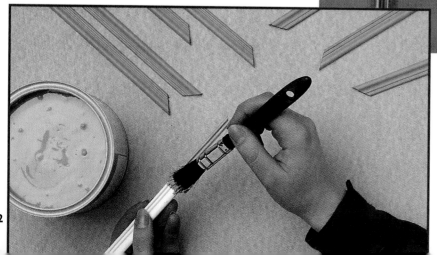

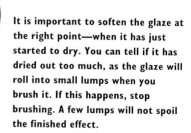

It is important to soften the glaze at the right point—when it has just started to dry. You can tell if it has dried out too much, as the glaze will roll into small lumps when you brush it. If this happens, stop brushing. A few lumps will not spoil the finished effect.

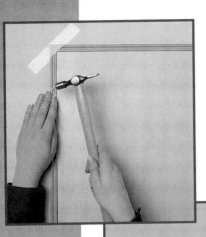

14 Attach the molding

● Attach the molding to the wall with finishing nails. Hold the molding in place with masking tape while you are hammering in the nails. If necessary, fill in any large gaps with wood filler and allow to dry.

16 Wood-grain horizontally

● Repeat steps 8–10 on the horizontal band of glaze. The technique is the same, except you are working horizontally. As you are combing across the wall, it is easier to remain standing so that you can walk as you work along the wall.

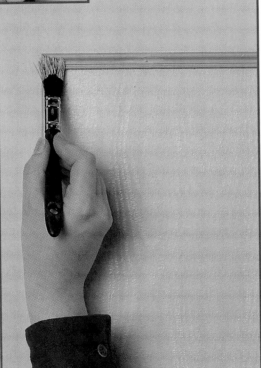

● Then touch up the corners of the panels and any nail hole marks with the dark green flat latex paint.

17 Apply the second band

● Once you have completed the wood-graining and combing on your first horizontal band of glaze, apply a second band of about the same width. Make sure you slightly overlap the first band of glaze.

18 Soften the glaze

● Take the softening brush and soften the join between the two bands, as well as the usual softening all over. Do not wait until you have covered the entire wall with glaze before softening it, as the glaze then will be too dry for the softening to work.

15 Glaze the wall

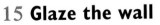

● When you have finished all the panels, paint a horizontal band of glaze about 6" wide on the wall below the chair rail. As with the panels, you should work in sections so that the glaze does not dry.

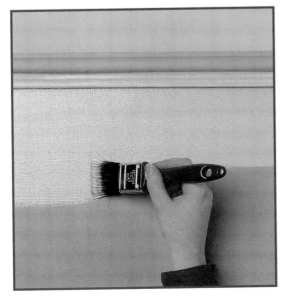

Lapis lazuli

Bring the glorious color of lapis lazuli into your home with this quick and easy technique. The deep blue of the precious mineral makes it ideal for any bathroom scheme.

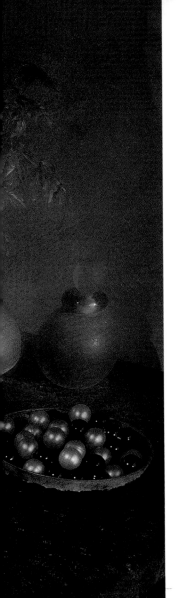

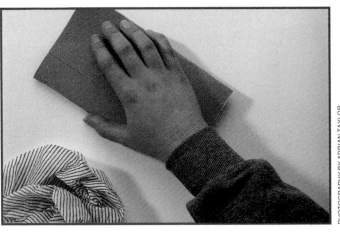

YOU WILL NEED:

- White oil-based paint
- Artist's oil colors in raw umber, coeruleum, French ultramarine and scarlet lake
- Gold embossing powder or gold powder paint
- Oil-based varnish
- Paint thinner
- Two 1½" paintbrushes
- Sword striper
- Medium-sized stencil brush
- Medium- and fine-grade sandpaper
- Lint-free cloth
- Plain white paper
- Three mixing bowls
- Mixing sticks

Lapis lazuli is a beautiful blue mineral, speckled with minute crystals of sparkling yellow pyrite, or "fool's gold." It was used as an inlay on Egyptian artifacts, and in medieval Europe it was ground into powder to create a spectacular sky blue pigment. This pigment was often used in religious paintings to color the Virgin Mary's mantle.

Today lapis lazuli is one of the most expensive and valued semi-opaque decorative materials in the world, and it is usually found carved into jewelry and small accessories, or as an inlaid detail on furniture. With the paint technique, however, you can be generous and use it over a large area such as a countertop. Authentic lapis lazuli can have understated veining and a subtle speckling of gold, but for the paint effect you can exaggerate these features. The technique is easy to follow and uses simple materials, but the finished effect is extravagant and sumptuous.

Materials

Artist's oil colors, mainly in two shades of blue, are ragged, stippled and spattered to create depth. To imitate yellow pyrite, sprinkle on gold powder or powder paint, available from art supply shops. For vertical areas such as walls, you can spatter with liquid leaf instead.

1 Preparation

● Sand the surface with medium-grade sandpaper and wipe clean, using a cloth dampened with paint thinner. This will provide a good surface for the paint.

2 Apply the base coat

● You will need two coats of oil-based paint to give a smooth surface. Apply the first coat and allow to dry for up to 16 hours. Sand with fine-grade sandpaper before applying a second coat. Wipe with a cloth dampened with paint thinner.

4 Stipple the surface

● Stipple the surface with the 1½" paint-brush to disperse the oil color. If you stipple away too much, simply add more of each color. Now is the time to adjust the shade, adding a touch more ultramarine to darken, or coeruleum for a lighter blue.

Color guide

The glorious blue of genuine lapis lazuli does vary in tone, so there are no hard-and-fast rules for the paint effect. On the bathroom counter, we used three times as much coeruleum as French ultramarine. The more French ultramarine you use, the darker the finished effect. Gold speckles are an intrinsic part of the mineral, but, again, you can vary the amount. If you are covering a large area, you can sprinkle generously. With veins, however, always err on the side of caution. Too many will detract from the color and speckled effect.

5 Rag the surface

● With a scrunched-up piece of paper, rag the surface to add texture. Some of the white base coat should show through. If you rag off too much, apply undiluted oil color and re-stipple with the paintbrush.

3 Dab on the oil colors

● Dab undiluted coeruleum and French ultramarine oil color all over the surface in random dots. Use about three times as much coeruleum as French ultramarine—the latter is very dark, and if you use too much, your lapis lazuli could look almost black.

6 Make up the glaze mixtures

● Squeeze a little coeruleum into a bowl and add paint thinner. Stir well until the color is evenly distributed. Mix up enough to vein and spatter the surface. Squeeze small amounts of scarlet lake and raw umber into separate bowls, add paint thinner and mix—you will need just enough of these colors for spattering.

7 Paint in the veins

● Load the sword striper with the diluted coeruleum and draw in a few veins at random diagonally across the surface. Make sure the veins do not cross over. Use this technique sparingly, however, as too many veins will ruin the finished effect.

8 Spatter the surface

● Load the stencil brush with the darkest glaze mixture (here, raw umber) and spatter. Repeat, using coeruleum and scarlet lake.

■ To spatter the glaze, load the stencil brush and tap its handle lightly against the 1½" paintbrush in a downward motion. Hold the brushes about 10" above the surface. Spatter onto a piece of scrap paper first to get rid of the largest dots of paint.

■ On vertical surfaces, gold powder can be difficult to apply, so use liquid leaf to imitate the pyrite crystals. Load an old toothbrush with the leaf then, holding the brush 4" to 6" away from the surface, run your index finger across the top of the bristles to create minute spatters (see Floating Marble, page 81).

■ When veining your surface, create a pattern in the manner of a lightning fork or twig—starting at a single point and building to a series of branches. The veins should never be allowed to cross one another, as crossing veins are never encountered in nature.

SEAN ELLIS

9 Sprinkle with gold

● Pour some gold powder into a bowl, take a pinch and sprinkle randomly over the surface. The powder will not adhere immediately, so wait until the surface is dry before blowing off any excess.

10 Apply the varnish

● When the surface is completely dry, apply a coat of varnish, adding further layers if it is likely to suffer a lot of wear and tear. Use an exterior varnish for greater protection. Allow to dry for up to 48 hours.

HELP FILE

■ If you want to lighten up the overall finish of your surface, you can spatter on a small amount of white oil color diluted with paint thinner.

■ Before applying a sprinkling of gold powder, take the dry sword striper and run it through the veins. This clears away any tiny dots of color from the spattering. They are dispersed through the veins, darkening them slightly.

SEAN ELLIS

Before

Lapis lazuli mirror

The faux lapis lazuli technique, so effective over a large surface, works equally well on small areas and objects. You can use it to embellish individual items or create a coordinated look with several small accessories complementing a larger panel; for example, a chest of drawers and dressing table set. Any flat surface will take the paint effect, as long as you prepare it properly.

For the mirror, the technique is just the same as the one used for the bathroom counter. In small areas, however, the veins and speckles will tend to appear magnified, so use them with restraint. You can vary the tones of the blue, but remember, if you choose a very dark shade combined with less gold and fewer veins, the finished effect may not have the same impact.

CHAPTER 3

Finishing Touches

A garden with walls that have no decoration or climbing plants can feel uninviting—but a new white statue can look equally stark. Follow these ten easy steps to create a subtly aged masterpiece that will look as if it has grown old gracefully.

Aging a
STATUE

BEFORE

A new, bright white plaster statue may look out of place when you first put it out in your garden. However, its rough relief is perfect for aging. You will be creating a patchy effect, using layers of white, creamy yellow, raw sienna and moss green, blended and worked to give a time-mellowed look. Choose a piece that is not too large to start with so that you get a feel for the technique.

E·QUIPMENT·

YOU WILL NEED:
- Small can of quick-drying acrylic primer
- Flat latex paint in creamy yellow
- Flat latex paint in bright white
- Artist's acrylic color in raw sienna
- Artist's acrylic color in yellow ocher
- Artist's acrylic color in moss green
- Acrylic varnish
- 2" paintbrush
- Toothbrush
- Sea sponge
- Cotton rag
- Mixing palette

The traditional way to add a mossy, aged effect to stoneware was to daub it with live yogurt culture and wait for the lichen to grow. But this took time. Now, using easy paint techniques, you can achieve a realistic aging effect—it is remarkably simple to do in just ten easy steps. This aging technique can be applied to any nonabsorbent matte surface—painting over gloss will not work. We have used a plaster wall motif, given it layers of latex paint and acrylic color, then applied green acrylic color to appear as moss.

There are several stages to the aging process, but even allowing time for drying, you can complete the effect in a day. You will need to apply seven coats, including the primer and varnish. Several of these layers need to dry completely before applying the next one; others need to be blended over each other for a softer effect.

The effect builds up with a combination of sponging, stippling and spattering techniques to produce a convincing appearance of lichen and moss—in a fraction of the normal time.

1 Prime the statue

- Before priming the statue, make sure there are no loose or flaking areas and that the surface is free from dirt, grease and wax. Using your paintbrush, apply a coat of acrylic primer all over the statue, then allow it to dry completely. This will take between 1 and 2 hours.

2 Apply the base coat

● Using a clean paintbrush, apply an even coat of creamy yellow latex paint to the statue. Allow to dry completely—this could take 1 or 2 hours, although you can speed up the process by leaving it in a warm place.

3 Prepare to paint

● Using a clean paintbrush, dip it into the white latex paint and dab the brush on a piece of cloth to remove the excess paint. Make sure that you have very little paint left on the brush, as you need to apply only a very thin layer of paint.

4 Apply the white paint

● Dab a thin and patchy layer of white latex paint all over the statue to give a blotchy cover. Allow to dry completely; clean the brush again.

5 Stipple with raw sienna

● Squeeze a dab of raw sienna artist's acrylic color into the palette and blend with a little water. Dip the brush into the mixture and wipe to remove excess paint. Stipple in patches with a light, dabbing movement, leaving some areas of the statue uncovered.

6 Blend the colors

● Dampen a cloth with a little water and dab it gently over the statue to blend the white latex paint with the raw sienna for a softer look.

7 Sponging in white

● Dampen the sponge with a little water, dip it in the white latex and dab off the excess paint on a cloth—the paint cover needs to be very sparse. Sponge the paint over the statue very lightly to give a speckled look that highlights the raised and exposed areas.

8 Prepare the colors

● Squeeze a dab of yellow ocher artist's acrylic into a clean palette, add a little water and mix together. Repeat the process, using the moss green acrylic.

9 Spatter with color

● Dip the toothbrush into the yellow ocher and spatter the color onto the statue by drawing your finger in a downward direction over the bristles so that fine spots of color are flicked onto the statue. Repeat with the moss green mixture, flicking in soft, random patches. You might like to spatter the moss green color mainly on one side of the cherub to give a realistic moss effect. Allow the paint to dry completely.

10 Water-based varnish

● Pour a little acrylic varnish into a bowl and using a clean brush, apply an even coat all over the statue. Allow to dry in a well-ventilated room for several hours or overnight. This will seal in the paintwork and protect the statue from weathering.

The finished effect

The effect you are aiming for is a natural, weathered look that makes the statue blend comfortably with its surroundings. Look at the natural patterns of moss and other features in the setting surrounding the statue and use them as a guide for aging.

Verdigris
GARDEN CHAIR

Use a simple stippling technique to imitate the gentle, blue-green shades of natural aging. In easy steps, discover how quickly you can give new life to furniture and accessories all around your home.

Natural verdigris—the soft green often seen on the domes of capital buildings—is the result of corrosion on metals, such as bronze; today, this aged look is in fashion, and you can use paint to imitate its chalky and harmonious colors. This easy dabbing technique can give an authentic aged look to almost any surface. We've transformed a garden chair that was past its prime and an inexpensive plastic plant pot with spectacular results.

1 Preparation

Although this garden chair—one of a set—was cracked and rusty, its ornate shape made it particularly suitable for an aged look. The seat is made of metal, and there is a molded plastic covering on the back; both need to be completely clean and smooth to ensure a perfect and lasting finish.

● If a metal surface is rusted, brush it until it is smooth (see Help File, right).

● To clean plastic surfaces, wash them carefully with a clean cloth and a solution of warm water and an all-purpose liquid cleanser or other household detergent.

● Rinse the chair thoroughly with clean water, then make sure it is completely dry before you continue.

2 Red oxide

To provide a good surface for painting, apply a base coat of red oxide metal primer. This is especially important for outdoor garden furniture, as it inhibits rust and protects the metal. This can be rather messy, and the red oxide base is hard to remove from clothes, so cover the floor with newspapers, wear old clothes and protect your hands with rubber gloves.

● Apply the primer to give an even, overall coating, then allow about 24 hours for it to dry thoroughly.

3 Base coat

Brush on the bronze-green base color with smooth strokes until the entire chair is evenly covered. Allow to dry. The flat-finish water-based paint dries quickly—in as little as 2 hours. If the first coat appears patchy, give the whole chair a second coat. The aim is to create a foundation of flat color as a base for the stippling.

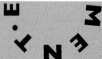

YOU WILL NEED:

● Small can of red oxide metal primer
● The smallest available can of dark brown-green flat latex paint for the base color
● One can each in the smallest available size of turquoise-green and pale green flat latex paint
(Or use a verdigris kit, such as the Paint Magic Verdigris Kit by Jocasta Innes or the Patina Antiquing Kit by Modern Options. Be sure to follow the manufacturer's instructions.)
● Small can of clear matte polyurethane varnish or a can of clear spray varnish
● 2" paintbrush
● Stippling brush
● Varnish brush
● Liquid detergent and cloth for cleaning
● Fine sandpaper or wire brush
● Newspaper
● Rubber gloves

4 Test the brush

The mottled verdigris effect is created by stippling in two colors over the base. To perfect your technique, practice first on paper. Pour a little turquoise-green paint into a saucer and dip the stippling brush into it to coat the ends of the bristles. Wipe off excess paint until the brush is nearly dry. Holding the brush upright, dab the tip onto the paper. The best effects come from using very little paint and dabbing quite firmly.

5 Turquoise stippling

Using the turquoise paint in the saucer, load your stippling brush with the right amount of paint and with a quick dabbing movement, stipple unevenly over the base to create a misting of color. Build up stippling in patches to imitate the real effect, making sure the base color shows through.

6 Pale green stippling

When the first color has dried, pour a little of the pale green paint into a saucer and repeat the process. The second color is lighter and brighter and helps build a soft, powdery look. Do not overdo the stippling—the first color and the base coat should show through. Check that you have covered the whole chair.

7 Varnishing

When the chair is completely dry, apply one or two coats of clear matte polyurethane varnish. This is particularly important for any outdoor garden furniture, as it seals and protects the paintwork and helps it withstand the inevitable wear and tear of use.

● If your chair is one of a set, repeat the whole process on each one—the paint quantities given are ample for four or more chairs. To complete the transformation, when the last coat of varnish is completely dry, add the finishing touch of new seat covers in colors to complement the blue-green verdigris.

PAINT QUANTITIES

Although you may need quite a large quantity of the base color, especially if you need to give your chosen item two coats, you need so little of the two green colors that you may find it more economical to blend the colors, using artist's water-based acrylic paints diluted with water to the consistency of latex paint. Coat with varnish in the same way as for latex paint. Being acrylic-based, these paints will not wash off. Poster paints, however, are not suitable.

SPRAY VARNISH

For items that are small or difficult to varnish with a brush, use a can of clear spray varnish and apply according to the manufacturer's instructions to give an even protective covering.

PAINTED PLANTERS

The colors of verdigris look particularly stunning when set off by the natural colors of plants and flowers. Plant pots and window boxes of all shapes and sizes can look beautiful with a verdigris finish.

WICKERWORK

Although it is ideal for metals and plastics, a verdigris finish gives almost any item an instant touch of class. Try it on inexpensive wicker furniture and baskets for some unusual and charming results.

VERSATILE FINISH

There is virtually no limit to the items all around the house that can take on a new lease on life with a verdigris finish.

Picture frames, candlesticks, lamp bases, old metal desk lights and wall brackets are ideal candidates, and as you get more experienced, you will develop an eye for what is suitable and how to achieve the most natural effects on each item. If you get the opportunity, look at the effect as it occurs naturally, and stipple in washy patches to imitate the clouded appearance of the real thing.

Plastic planter

Inexpensive plastic urns are available from your local garden center or general hardware store. The dramatic transformation on this planter took less than two days, allowing time for the red oxide to dry. The finished urn looks like an expensive classical bronze urn, with the green verdigris colors set off

perfectly by bright summer flowers and trailing foliage. Follow the steps as for the chair. If the urn is smooth, rub it down with sandpaper before painting with red oxide metal primer so that the paint will adhere properly. If the urn is going to be kept outdoors, make sure that it is well sealed with several coats of varnish to protect it against the effects of water and wear.

LEAVES
on a tray

Select a handful of perfect leaves and use them to create unique and elegant designs. The technique is a simple one of reverse stenciling—the leaves provide perfect cutout shapes for you to use for your own patterns and projects.

PHOTOGRAPHY BY ADRIAN TAYLOR

BEFORE

● With a little imagination and some paint colors, you can turn a plain tray into a uniquely designed accessory.

YOU WILL NEED:
● Freshly picked ivy leaves
● Satin-finish oil-based paint in aqua, French navy and sage
● Artist's acrylic color in leaf green
● 8 oz matte acrylic varnish
● Two small paintbrushes, about ¾"
● Small sea sponge
● Small artist's brush
● Masking tape
● Scissors
● Saucer

Use simple sponging over a pattern of leaves laid out on a tray to give a reverse stenciled image. It is a quick technique, ideal for small items, as you can vary the size and spacing of your motifs much more easily than with a precut stencil.

Materials

Use satin latex paint for a finish with a slight sheen and an impermeable surface. Provided the object you want to paint is completely clear of dirt and grease, satin latex will adhere to almost any surface, forming an ideal base for sponging. Unlike satin oil-based paint, the oil-based equivalent, satin latex dries in about four hours for speedy results, and you can clean brushes with water.

Shapes and colors

Select fifteen to thirty leaves of varying sizes, according to the proportions of the item you want to decorate. Make sure that some have stems to use in a trailing leaf pattern.

Color combinations can be as varied as you like, but to be in keeping with the leaf motifs, try shades of green and blue, or rustic autumn browns and golds. Just as with color combinations for sponging on walls, you can combine shades of one color for a harmonious tone-on-tone effect, or you can introduce bolder contrasts for a more eye-catching look.

The tray makeover requires very little paint—use a color left over from decorating a room, with colors for sponging that pick out elements of upholstery or furnishings.

1 Preparation

● Wash the tray thoroughly to remove any traces of dirt or grease; dry well. Using a small brush, apply a coat of aqua latex paint to cover the top and sides of the tray. Allow to dry completely (about 2–4 hours), then turn upside down and paint the outer sides of the tray to match.
● Cut a small strip of masking tape and double it back on itself to make a double-sided sticky loop. (If available, you could use double-sided adhesive tape.) Press this loop onto the back of a leaf, taking care that the tape does not extend

beyond the edge of the leaf itself. Repeat for all the leaves—if they are large, you will need more than one piece of tape on the back of each leaf to hold them flat on the tray. Set aside the leaves, tape-side up. If any of the leaves curl or crack, discard and replace them with perfect ones.

2 Position the leaves

● Place the leaves so that they rest lightly on the tray in a trailing pattern with the largest ones positioned at the the start of the trail and graduating down in size toward the tip. Angle the leaves so that they form three sprays that flow over the sides. When you are happy with the design, press the leaves firmly in place.

3 Sponge the surface

● Pour a little of the navy paint into a saucer; dilute with a little water so that it is like thick cream but not as runny as for normal sponging. Dab the sponge in the paint, wipe off the excess, then use to sponge all over the top and inner sides of the tray to give a densely

speckled effect.
● When dry, repeat the same procedure, sponging over the top with the sage latex paint.

4 Remove the leaves

● When the sponging is completely dry, lift the edge of one of the leaves and holding it down lightly with the other hand, peel back the leaf and masking tape, taking care not to lift off the background paint. Repeat, removing all the leaves to reveal the leaf pattern across the tray.

5 Paint the stems

● If any sponged paint has seeped under the leaves, touch up the edges with a little aqua paint on an artist's brush. Still using the aqua paint, paint on a trailing stem with stalks, attaching the leaves to it. If you like, add some curling tendrils as additional decoration.

● Take care that the leaves are stuck completely flat onto the surface of the tray, and load the sponge sparingly so that paint does not seep underneath the leaves. If the newly picked leaves are too springy, leave overnight in a cool place so that they wilt and soften a little.

6 Add the leaf veins

● Using the sage latex paint diluted with a little water, lightly paint in the veins on each leaf outline, following the way the veins run from your template leaves. Start with a line from the base of the leaf almost to the central point, then from a lower point along this vein, add branching veins to the other points of the leaf. If you make any slips at this stage, either wipe it off while it is still wet and start again, or you can wait until the sage paint dries and cover up the mistake using aqua paint on an artist's brush.

7 Varnish the tray

● When the paint is completely dry, use a small brush to cover the top and inner sides of the tray with water-based varnish. When this is dry, turn the tray over and varnish the base and outer sides. For extra protection, repeat to give a double coating of varnish, drying thoroughly between coats.

Umbrella stand

Add a tumbling of autumn leaves in rusty orange and brown on an umbrella stand. Choose horse chestnut leaves in different sizes and apply them randomly over the sides of the painted stand, then sponge and add details as for the tray.

AUTUMN PATTERNS

Prepare the umbrella stand by sanding and cleaning, then apply a base coat of orange satin latex paint. Position the leaves, using several loops of tape for larger leaves, then sponge over the dry base, using first a rich brown and then terra-cotta. Fill in the veins on the leaves in terra-cotta, then finish, when dry, with two coats of varnish.

TRAY IDEAS

The reverse stencil design is just as effective using different tray shapes or other types of leaves. Try nasturtium, oak or maple leaves for unusual shapes and arrange the leaves in patterns to complement the shape of the tray.

Stenciled table

Use paint thinner and stenciling crayons to transform a plain table with gentle colors and an aged pattern.

Before

Add a gently aged look to furniture and accessories with this quick and easy stenciling technique. Using paint thinner and stenciling crayons, you can transform plain items, such as this old side table. Create a lightly mottled background by spraying paint on the tabletop through tapestry canvas, then stencil and distress motifs over the top. You do not need any artistic skills—paint thinner breaks up the stencil color and does all the work for you.

First steps

Stenciling crayons are easy to use. As they are oil-based, they take longer to dry than water-based paints, giving you more time to blend and blur the colors to soften.

Pale, neutral tones, such as soft cream, are ideal for the oil base and are suitable for most schemes. For best results, use similar tones of one color for both the background and stenciling.

Select a stencil design to complement the style of the item you plan to decorate or use one from the Stencil Collection.

PHOTOGRAPHY BY ADRIAN TAYLOR

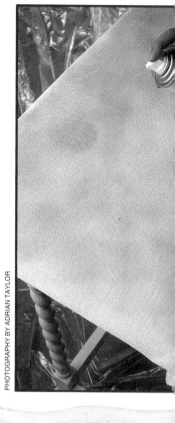

YOU WILL NEED:

EQUIPMENT.

- Oil-based paint in cream
- Spray paint in blue and beige
- Oil-based stenciling crayons in white and two shades of blue
- Matte oil-based varnish
- Paint thinner
- Paintbrush
- Stencil brush
- Medium-sized artist's brush
- Fine artist's brush
- Fine tapestry canvas

- Stencil acetate
- Spray adhesive
- Medium-grade and fine-grade sandpaper
- Lint-free cloth
- Drop cloth
- Masking tape
- Scissors
- Plain white paper
- Pen
- Cutting mat
- Craft knife
- Plastic plate
- Bowl

1 Prepare the surface

- Sand the surface with medium- and then fine-grade sandpaper. Dampen a cloth with paint thinner and wipe away any dust or grease from the surface.

2 Paint on the base color

- Apply an even layer of cream oil-based paint over the whole table and allow to dry for 12–14 hours. If necessary, apply a second coat to give a solid, even cover.

134

3 Spray through the canvas

● Lay a drop cloth on the floor and run some masking tape around the lip of the table. Stretch the fine tapestry canvas over the tabletop and secure with masking tape. Spray in light strokes with blue spray paint until you have a mottled texture, and then add a few touches of beige spray paint. Remove the tapestry canvas and allow the paint to dry for about 1 hour.

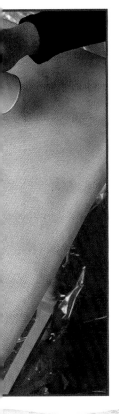

4 Prepare a stencil

● Draw your designs on a sheet of plain paper, then place the stencil acetate on top. Secure both to the cutting mat with masking tape and cut a stencil with the craft knife by following the designs underneath (see Cutting Your Own Stencil, page 137).

5 Stencil in blue

● Separate the the two stencil motifs and spray the back of the larger motif with spray adhesive. Position it at the edge of the table, roughly in the middle. Rub a little of each stenciling stick onto the plastic plate and load the stencil brush from this. Stencil the design, blending the colors to give a gentle shading.

TIPS

■ Try to keep the surface you are working on flat; otherwise, the paint thinner may run and spoil the overall pattern and design.

■ To protect the legs from the spray paint, skirt the table with a drop cloth held in place with masking tape.

■ To repair any blemishes on the textured background, mask off around the affected area with scrap paper so that the rest of the table is protected. Place a piece of tapestry canvas over the unmasked area and spray on blue and beige color, as before.

■ If when you remove the tapestry canvas, you are not satisfied with the background texture, secure the canvas back in place and spray on some more color.

■ Instead of drawing a stencil design from scratch, trace an image or pattern from a piece of fabric or wallpaper and use as the basis for your stencil.

6 Blur the stencil color

● While the stencil color is still wet, pour some paint thinner into a bowl and using the medium-sized artist's brush, dab generously over the stenciled design to blur the edges and the color. Continue blotting with the artist's brush until the design has a gently mottled texture. Repeat the stenciling and blurring until the whole design is finished.

7 Add white shading

● Rub some of the white stencil color onto the plastic plate and dab with a tiny amount of paint thinner to dilute it. Using the fine artist's brush, gently add a little shading around the outline of each stencil design. Allow to dry for at least 10 hours.

8 Finishing touches

● Remove all the masking tape, load the stencil brush with some blue paint and gently stipple the color around the lip of the table. Then load the medium-sized artist's brush with paint thinner and dab generously over the blue to mottle it. Repeat on the legs and allow to dry for at least 10 hours.

9 Apply varnish

● Once the surface is completely dry, coat with at least two layers of matte oil-based varnish, allowing 12–14 hours for each layer to dry.

! Do not be tempted to rush the stenciling and blurring. Oil-based stencil colors take several hours to dry, and the paint thinner will blur the design as long as the stencil colors are not completely dry.

Stenciling ideas

Brighten up accessories with this simple and versatile stenciling technique.

Garden basket

Transform a plain wooden basket with bright colors and a combination of ordinary and reverse stenciling. Over a base of cream oil paint, stencil your design in a deep crimson. Cut a second design from paper and stick in position with reusable adhesive. Blend reds and pinks over the whole surface, including the paper stencils, with a stencil brush and blur gently with paint thinner.

Tea tray

The country colors of red and white are perfect for this pretty tray. To imitate the pattern, split your stencil into smaller sections by masking off the parts you do not wish to use. This is much quicker and easier than designing and cutting several coordinating stencils.

Cutting your own stencil is easy—just copy or adapt your chosen motif. Once you know how, the possibilities are endless. A boldly colored fabric was the inspiration for this bright two-part stencil—just follow the simple steps to cut a stencil and create a colorful jungle in a child's room.

CUTTING YOUR OWN

stencil

YOU WILL NEED:

- One bottle each of water-based stencil paint in red, yellow, black and two shades of green
- Can of spray varnish
- Foam sponge
- Large sheet of stencil acetate
- Indelible marker
- Cutting mat
- Craft knife with replaceable blade
- Scissors
- Artist's tape
- Masking tape

E·Q·U·I·P·M·E·N·T·

Stenciling is a simple and fun way to decorate your home and give an instant touch of fun to any room. Making your own stencil is easy—up-to-date equipment makes adapting and cutting precise designs quick and simple.

You need the design for your stencil to have a good, bold outline—motifs taken from wallpaper or curtain fabric are ideal for accessorizing a room. We have used a leopard taken from a jungle fabric to make a two-part stencil to decorate furniture in a child's room.

For a one-part stencil, you need to choose a design that has no pattern within the windows of the cut stencil—it is impossible to include a "floating" design within a stencil. If you make a two-part stencil, however, you can add pattern and detail in a precise position over the top of your main design.

Using stencil acetate

Craft shops sell sheets of acetate specially designed for cutting stencils. This durable plastic is semi-transparent, so it allows you to trace outlines straight through. (For details of how to make a stencil the more traditional way, using cardboard and tracing paper, see Help File, right.) When you first make a stencil, use a craft knife; later, if you find you are cutting a lot of stencils, it is worth investing in an electric stencil cutter, which works by melting the acetate (this is unsuitable for cutting cardboard). Just follow the simple steps and use your tailor-made stencil to add color and style to walls and furnishings, such as lampshades, roller blinds, cupboards or drawers. When you can make a stencil from any design—or part of a design—the possibilities for accessorizing all around your home are endless.

1 Draw the first stencil

● Iron the fabric and lay it on a flat surface. Cut a piece of acetate at least 1¼" larger all around than the chosen design. Position the acetate over the motif and secure it on each side, using artist's tape. Trace the outline of the motif, drawing on the acetate with the indelible marker. To avoid weak spots on the stencil, do not cut any bridges narrower than ⅛" in width.

2 The second stencil

● To make the second stencil, cut another piece of acetate, position it over the motif and secure with tape. The first stencil represents the solid elements of the motif—the head and body. The second stencil creates the details—in this case, the leopard's features and spots. Using the indelible marker, outline the motif with a dotted line. This is important for positioning the second stencil over the first. Then clearly outline all the details that appear within the main outline.

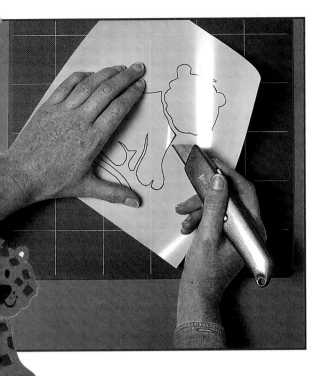

3 Cut the first stencil

● Starting with the first stencil, place the acetate on a cutting mat or piece of glass with taped edges. Use a craft knife with a sharp, replaceable blade to cut along the lines of the design. Hold down the stencil with one hand and take the knife firmly in the other hand. To avoid ragged outlines, cut in one smooth action, using your whole arm and taking care not to lift the knife from the cutting board. Rotate the acetate stencil—not the mat or the knife—as you cut firmly along the lines. You should find that you scarcely vary the angle at which you cut. The first stencil is complete when you have cut out the shapes of the head and body.

4 Cut the second stencil

● To cut the second stencil, lay the acetate on the mat and hold it down with one hand; take the cutting knife in the other hand and cut out the shapes of the details and features. Ignore the dotted outline—this is only there to help you when you position the second stencil over the first for stenciling.

Carefully cut out all the shapes within the dotted line—by now, you should be cutting with confidence. Make sure you cut out each shape in one smooth action, rotating the stencil, not the mat, as you go. This is particularly important when you come to cut out the more intricate shapes, such as the features of the face.

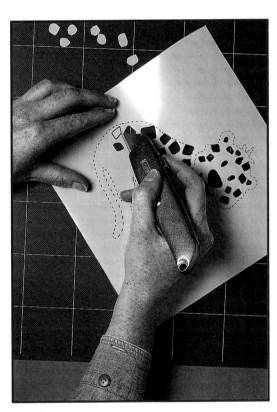

HELP FILE

■ **USING TRACING PAPER AND CARDBOARD**
If you are unable to find stencil acetate, you can make a stencil the traditional way, using tracing paper and cardboard. Lay the ironed fabric on a flat surface, place a sheet of tracing paper over the motif and tape down. Then, with a soft pencil, draw around the

outline of the motif. Cut a square of cardboard, then flip the tracing paper and tape it to the cardboard, penciled outline down. Using a soft pencil, scribble over the outline to transfer it to the cardboard. When you remove the tracing paper, the motif will be outlined on the cardboard. Follow the same procedure for the second stencil, this time tracing the details inside the motif, as in step 2. Cut out, as in steps 3 and 4. Remember, this makes a mirror image of the motif. Flip the stencil over so that the leopard is facing the original way, as on the fabric.

TIPS

with paint. Always dab off any excess paint on scrap paper before you start to stencil.

■ If you overcut or tear the stencil while cutting it out, repair the broken bridge using masking tape on both sides. Trim it flush with a craft knife.

■ Stenciling with a sponge is quick and easy, but be careful not to overload the sponge

■ Make sure that the first stencil is completely dry before you add the details. Stencil paints cover each other easily when dry, but if you start the second stencil while the first is still wet, you will end up with muddy-looking blended colors and may smudge the first stencil.

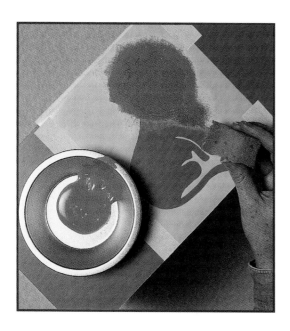

5 Stencil the first color

● Remove the top drawer from the bureau and take off the handles. Work out how many motifs you wish to stencil and how you want to position them. Attach the stencil to the drawer front with masking tape. Pour a little yellow paint into a saucer and load a small piece of sponge. Stencil the head and body of the lion.

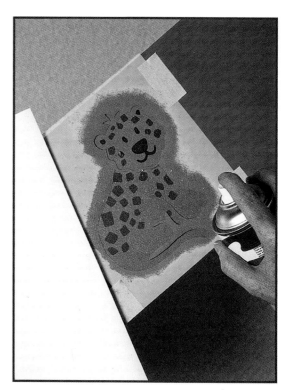

6 Position the details

● When the first stenciled motif is completely dry, attach the second stencil so that the dotted out-line of the body fits exactly over the first stenciled shape below it. Stick the stencil in place with masking tape on each side and pour a little red and black stencil paint into two saucers.

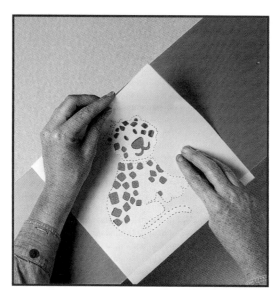

8 Spray with varnish

● When the stencils are dry, position the first stencil over the motif, secure with tape and spray the whole motif with varnish, using a sheet of paper to protect the drawer surface. Replace the handles.

▼ Once you have mastered cutting a stencil, expand the idea further by stenciling secondary items. To decorate a lampshade, we cut a leaf stencil from acetate, using a design from the fabric, then stenciled it in two colors to frame the face of the leopard.

7 Stencil the details

● Cut two fresh pieces of sponge and load one with red paint. Use this to stencil in the spots of the leopard. Load the other piece of sponge with black paint and stencil in the face and ears of the leopard. If you think that you may carry black paint onto the spots, mask off the surrounding windows with masking tape, then finish the stenciling in black.

Stencil outlines

▼ Designs with strong, simple motifs are ideal for cutting your first stencil, as they can be translated easily into one- or two-part stencils. The jungle fabric from which we took our designs offers plenty of possibilities of animals and foliage. If you particularly like this design, you can use the outlines on this page to cut your own stencil.

You may already have some fabric from which you would like to take one or two simple stencil motifs. Once you start to look at fabrics, you'll see that this is an idea with infinite possibilities and potential.

SIMPLE BORDERS

A border design can be used in all kinds of adventurous ways to add interest and drama to your home. These simple border stencils make a versatile addition to your collection and can transform walls, furniture and accessories.

EQUIPMENT

YOU WILL NEED:
- Simple Borders stencil from the Stencil Collection
- Stencil paints
- Stencil brushes, household sponge or foam sponge pieces
- Spray adhesive
- Cutting mat
- Ruler
- Set square
- Craft knife
- Paper
- Masking tape
- Scissors
- Palette

B order stencils can be used in a multitude of ways. As well as adding interest to walls, these border designs can add a personal touch to chair backs, mirrors, picture frames and shelves—in fact, all kinds of furniture and accessories can be given a new lease on life with a cleverly applied border.

To get the most from these border designs, it is important to know how to cope with corners. We'll show you some different ways of achieving this, along with the best technique for carrying the pattern around the corners of a room. Following these steps will give your border stenciling a really professional finish.

Planning

If you are stenciling horizontal borders around a room, you need to mark the wall with level guidelines. These mark the point where you should position the bottom of the stencil. Measure a fixed distance down from the ceiling or up from the baseboard at both ends of your wall and mark these points with chalk.

Unroll some cord over a piece of chalk in your hand to coat it, and pin on the wall so that it is taut. Gently lift the cord away from the wall and allow it to twang back. The impact of the cord hitting the wall will leave a perfectly straight chalk line.

Preparing the stencil

Mounting the sides of your chosen border stencil with paper can make it easier to handle across a whole wall.

1 Divide the stencil sheet

● Place the stencil on the cutting mat and neatly divide into three. Make sure you cut through the middle of the space between the designs so that each has a manageable border area around it.

2 Mount with paper

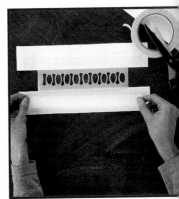

● Cut a couple of fairly wide strips of paper and place these under the upper and lower sides of the stencil so that the edge of the paper just overlaps the edge of the acetate. Secure in place with masking tape.

3 Trim the edges

● Trim the edges of the paper so that the ends align with the end of the acetate. Paper-mounted border stencils should only be used on a straight run of wall, not when approaching or negotiating around corners—for this, you will need to use an unmounted stencil so that it is as maneuverable and flexible as possible.

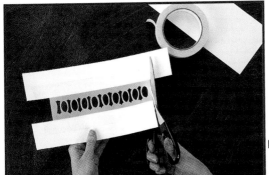

Symmetrical border patterns can be adapted to work around corners. You can do this either by turning the design at right angles and matching it to the existing stenciling, as shown on the chair, above, and the wall design, left—or by mitering the corner and masking off a diagonal half of it as you stencil each side of the angle so that the two fit together to form a matching right angle. Choose whichever method is most suitable for the type of design you are using.

Dealing with corners of walls

Stenciling a border design around a corner of a room is easy—you just need to make sure that you press the stencil acetate tightly into the corner, and that the pattern will continue along an even horizontal line on the next wall.

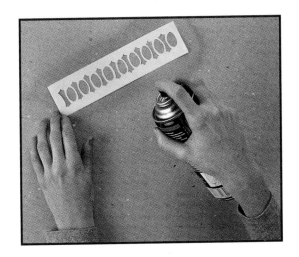

> Where a corner is between two unbroken walls, start stenciling in the corner and work outward to end naturally at a window or a door.

1 Spray with adhesive

● Spray your stencil lightly with adhesive so that you can attach it firmly and closely into the angle of the corner.

2 Position the stencil

● Using the end motifs of the last section of completed border as a guide, position the stencil so that its middle section fits neatly into the corner.

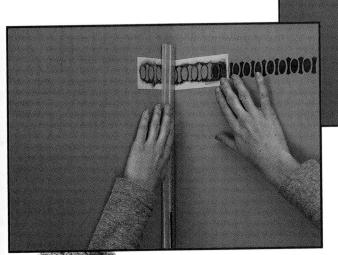

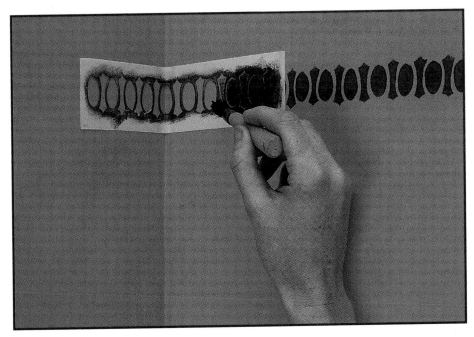

3 Push into the corner

● You need to stencil right into the corner, so use a ruler to push the stencil firmly but gently into the corner and press down securely. Make sure the design follows the marked line on the wall on the other side of the corner.

4 Stencil around the corner

● Stencil into the corner, taking care not to dab the bristles of the brush under the bridges of the stencil on the side of the angle next to where you are stenciling. If necessary, hold the acetate to the wall with your fingers for a better contact.

HELP FILE

■ A mirror tile is useful for seeing what a mitered corner will look like before you start stenciling. Stand the mirror on the stencil at the point in the pattern you want to form the corner, then look at the mirror image to see how the continuation of the corner will look. You can move the mirror up and down the design to view different corner effects.

■ Wavy, plantlike designs are particularly suitable for blocking out or filling in shapes so that the design fits a curve comfortably.

■ If you are stenciling a border around a wall, start your border in a relatively inconspicuous place—you will become more confident with the stencil as you proceed, and your technique will improve.

■ To stencil a border around a doorframe, you can mark a diagonal line in chalk coming out of the corners of the frame and carefully stencil up to the first of these. Pivot the stencil around the corner and continue stenciling, taking care not to pass the chalk line.

■ If your walls are uneven, do not position a border near the top, as this will emphasize the unevenness. If you position the border in the middle of the wall, wall defects will not be as noticeable.

Mitered corners

With a mitered corner, the horizontal and vertical patterns meet at right angles along a common diagonal line. Take care that the meeting patterns match each other exactly— if you follow these steps, you should get a neat and professional-looking corner.

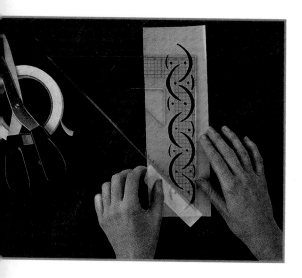

1 Choose the diagonal line

● Select a point on the pattern that will work neatly as a corner. (One way of visualizing this is to use a mirror; see Help File, page 145.) Using a set square as a guide, place a strip of masking tape diagonally across the pattern at the point where you want to miter it, toward the end of the stencil.

2 Start to stencil

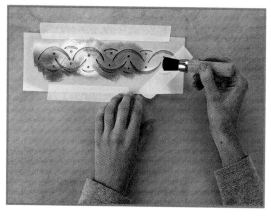

● Secure the stencil in place with masking tape and stencil right up to the diagonal tape. With this design of dots and curves, color blending is particularly effective in creating an impression of movement.

3 Flip the stencil

● Remove the stencil, and when the paint is completely dry, flip it over and apply another strip of masking tape to mask the other side of the diagonal line (remove the first strip of diagonal tape). Using the set square, align the flipped stencil vertically so that the taped end matches the edge of the horizontal border. Secure with masking tape.

4 Finish the corner

● Carefully peel off the stencil to reveal the corner. If you find that the two sides do not match up exactly, you can use a fine artist's brush and a little stencil paint to fill in any gaps in the stenciled motif.

This versatile design with its ropes, tassels and rosettes makes an easy highlight for walls or much smaller items. Find out how to connect the elements for an elegant and adaptable decoration.

ROPES & tassels

There are so many creative ways to use this linking rope and tassel stencil. We have used it to feature a collection of favorite plates, highlighting them with festooned ropes and tassels, and to trim a curtain tieback. In each case, the stencils are easy to position, quick to work and can be done in colors to match or complement any room scheme, and in the case of the plates, to show off any collection at its very best.

Framing a plate collection

The important thing when stenciling a geometrical design, such as this frame of ropes and tassels, is to ensure that the effect is absolutely symmetrical. All the ropes must hang vertically with no hint of a slant—this would spoil the trompe l'oeil deception that these are real ropes, hanging naturally on the wall. We'll show you all the tricks for getting the positioning just right—follow the easy steps for a perfect result.

Preliminaries

Before you start, make sure your wall is completely clean. It is not necessary to repaint if the finish is still good and, above all, has no marks, but the wall must be free of grease and dirt. Next, it is important to position your plates where they look best—remember that the draped ropes need space all around them to do justice to your collection. Once you have decided where to put them, you can start planning the stenciling.

Even if you are a very experienced stenciler, it can often help to try a practice motif to test how different colors look together—this could save time and re-stenciling later. Remember, too, that even if you blur your stenciling or use the wrong color, you can remedy it easily after the paint has dried.

YOU WILL NEED:
● **Rope and tassel stencil**
● **One 1-oz bottle each of water-based stencil paint in three shades of blue**
● **Foam sponge pieces or three stencil brushes (size 6 or 8)**
● **Pencil**
● **Large sheet of light cardboard**
● **Scissors**
● **Reusable adhesive**
● **Plumb line**
● **Masking tape or low-tack spray adhesive**
● **Tape measure**

1 Planning

● Draw circles around the plates on cardboard and cut out. Mark the center of each one. Position these roughly where you want them on the wall, sticking them in place with reusable adhesive. About 6" above the top plate, attach a plumb line with masking tape to hang through the center point of the

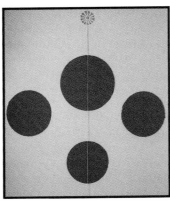

middle plates.
● Position the rosette immediately below the top of the plumb line; stencil, using brushes or pieces of sponge and using a separate piece or brush for each shade of paint.

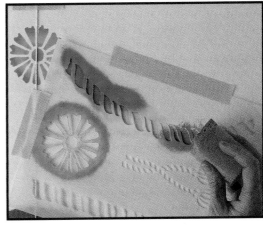

2 The first curved rope

● Attach the curved rope stencil at the right side of the rosette, slanting it so that the lower end lies roughly in line above the center right-hand plate. Stencil the rope in three shades of blue. Make a note of the distance between the lower end of the stenciled rope and the floor or top of the baseboard, and the horizontal distance between the plumb line and the end of the curved rope stencil.

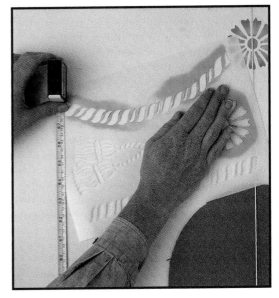

3 Position the left rope

● Measure the same horizontal distance left of the plumb line and the same vertical distance up from the floor or baseboard. Flip the curved rope stencil and position the lower end of it where the two measurements meet, with the upper end abutting the rosette on the lower left side.
● Stencil the rope as before, blending the three shades of blue.

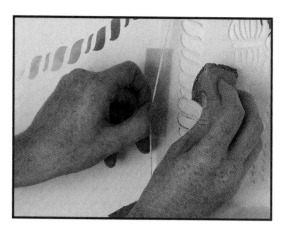

4 Stencil the center rope

● Stencil a rosette at the end of each curved rope. Attach the straight rope stencil below the center rosette in line with the plumb line. Lift off the cardboard rounds to stencil a continuous straight line, finishing just above the bottom of the lower plate.
● Repeat, hanging the plumb line from the center of the side rosettes, to stencil a straight rope on each side, ending above the bottom of the plates.

5 Stencil the tassels

● Replace the cardboard rounds to check the positioning; still using the plumb line, stencil the hanging tassels below each of the three lower plates, removing the cardboard rounds as you go. Make sure that the top of each will be concealed when the plates are in position.
● When the stenciling is dry, hang your plates in position, as planned.

 For stenciling on fabric, make sure the paint you use is suitable. Some stencil paints specify that they are for use on hard surfaces only, and some are specifically designed for use on fabric. There are some, however, that are suitable for both, and this is ideal for the curtain tieback where you need to use the same color on the wall and fabric.

Stencil a curtain tieback

1 Center motif

● Choose a firm-weave fabric for the tiebacks. Wash the fabric and press well. Cut four symmetrical templates the shape of the tieback out of firm cardboard, cutting two to be ½" smaller all around.
● Attach the stencil to a piece of scrap fabric and practice stenciling, applying paint very sparingly.

2 Cover the tieback

● Place one large template on the back of the fabric so that the straight grain runs horizontally across the template. Draw around the template on the fabric ⅝" from the edge to allow for turning. Cut out the fabric and use to cover the template, pleating the fabric to fit it closely around the curved edges. Glue in place with fabric glue or all-purpose glue. Make two loops, using soft cord. Make a hole 1" from each end of a small template and feed the cord through so that a 1" loop stands out at each end. Stick the small template over the back of the tieback. Turn the tieback over and position the rosette stencil so that it overlaps the end, as shown above. Stencil the partial rosette and repeat on the other end.

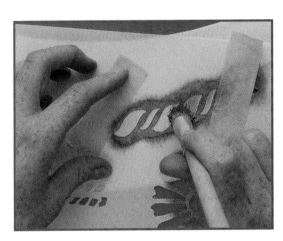

3 Stencil the center rope

● Mark a faint pencil or chalk mark down the center of the tieback, and use the curved rope stencil to work along it. You will need to keep repositioning the stencil at 2" or 2 ½" intervals, as shown above, to give a gentle curve that follows the line of the tieback. Work along the tieback, taking care not to smudge the paint as you move the stencil. ▲

4 Stencil the tieback edges

● Position the curved rope stencil so that it half overlaps the edge of the tieback and stencil a half-motif along the curved edges. As for the center motif, you will need to reposition the stencil to follow an even curve.
● Repeat along the top edge of the tieback to form a complete border all around it.

5 Position the wall rosette

● Make sure the wall is completely clean and dry. Mark the position where you want to attach the tieback and holding the end of it in place, attach the rosette stencil to the wall so that when hung from the loop from the center of the rosette on the wall, it exactly matches the stencil on the tieback. You may need to position it around the curtain to do this accurately.

6 Stencil the tassels

● Stencil the whole rosette, then when dry, add the tassels, making sure they hang vertically from the center of the rosette, as shown on the left.
● To attach the tieback to the wall, attach a small self-adhesive picture hook to the center of the rosette on the wall. Fold the tieback around the curtain and hang it on the hooks by the loops at either end. Repeat the whole process for the second tieback.

Your elegant cat stencil will
add a homey touch to
shelves, cushions, notebooks,
binders and more. Reverse
the stencil and your choice
of colors for the main
body and details
to create a clever
contrast. There's
also the chance
to try some
freehand work
when you
paint a border
around a
finished design.

A SITTING cat

YOU WILL NEED:

- Sitting Cat stencil from the Stencil Collection
- Water-based stencil paints
- Stencil brush
- Fine artist's brushes
- Palette
- Pencil
- Masking tape
- Scissors
- Gold-paint pen
- Sequins, stars and stickers
- White glue
- Thick cardboard

Cat shelf

A simply drawn stencil with clean, well-defined lines is sometimes the most effective, and this sitting cat lends itself to all kinds of embellishments. The motif is perfect for use on a wall or shelf, but can also be used to create homemade gifts, such as pictures with hand-painted borders or boldly decorated notebooks for children. Choose a single paint color for a stunning silhouette, or for a contrast, mix and match the shades used for the details—the ears, eyes, nose, mouth and bow. Remember to allow each layer of color to dry completely before starting on the next. Reverse the stencil to make a pair of cats and use opposite colors for the body and details on each. For a more opulent-looking result on gifts and cushion covers, replace the stenciled bow with a "jewel-encrusted" collar, using beads, sequins and a gold-paint pen.

1 Mark the shelf position

● Run the tip of a sharp pencil lightly along the top of your chosen shelf to mark its position, then remove the top of the shelf.

153

2 Position the stencil

● Position the stencil so that the cat's tail sits where the top of the shelf will be, and so that the stencil is straight. Secure in four places with pieces of masking tape.

3 Stipple the body

● Mix a paint color and fill in the head, body and tail, using a stencil brush. If you are stenciling a pair of cats, reverse the stencil and repeat steps 2 and 3.

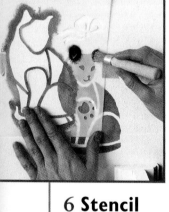

4 Position the face

● When the paint is completely dry, position the cat's face and fix in place with masking tape.

5 Stencil the face

● Choose or mix a contrasting shade and add the ears, eyes, nose and mouth, using a clean stencil brush. For a pair of cats, reverse the stencil and repeat on the other cat.

6 Stencil the bow

● Position the bow and fix the stencil in place. Using a clean stencil brush, fill in the bow. For a pair of cats, reverse the stencil and repeat on the other cat.

Kids' notebooks

Brighten up your child's school notebooks with a brilliant neon cat. If you're unsure whether the paint will adhere to the material, test the paw print on the inside or back of the notebook first. Protect the finished design by covering the notebook with clear self-adhesive film. You can do the same with school books (teachers permitting!), but cover them with suitable paper first. Again, protect the design with a layer of self-adhesive film.

1 Stencil the body

● Center the stencil on the front of the notebook and secure it with masking tape. Choose a paint color and fill in the cat's body, using a stencil brush.

2 Position the face

● When the body is completely dry, position the cat's face and fix in place with masking tape. Using a contrasting shade, fill in the ears, eyes, nose and mouth with a clean stencil brush.

Cushions

Using fabric paints, you can also use your versatile cat stencil to continue the theme around your home. Decorate plain cushion covers and soft furnishings with a simple silhouette or with one of the more glittery ideas (see below). Finish with a border of ribbon or binding.

3 Peel off the stencil

● Carefully lift the stencil from one edge and peel back gently, taking care not to smudge your work. Allow the paint to dry.

5 Decorate the finished design

● Decorate the finished design by sticking on some decorative stickers or sequins, beads and buttons. (Use white nontoxic glue for children's books and notebooks). If you haven't used the bow from the stencil, add a jewel-studded collar for a glamorous finishing touch.

4 Add a border

● Using a gold-paint pen or a fine brush, draw a freehand border all around the cat. It doesn't have to be sophisticated, as long as it's straight.

HELP FILE

THE CAT'S FACE

The stencil has been designed for you to position the cat's features so that he is looking to the right with his body facing left, or to the left with his body facing right. To achieve this, align the shorter side of his mouth with the outside edge of his face. If you prefer, you can center the features to change the angle of his gaze.

STENCILING ON FABRIC

Smooth fabrics absorb paint better than some textured ones, so test your chosen fabric first. Don't be put off if a ridged or heavily textured fabric doesn't seem to take the paint—persevere in layers, leaving the stencil in position between each coat, and you should find that the coverage builds up gradually.

COVERING SCHOOLBOOKS

If you are planning to cover and stencil your child's notebooks, test the paper first, as some papers tend to wrinkle and crease when they get wet—the matte side of thick brown paper usually gives good results.
Allow to dry completely, then cover with clear self-adhesive film.

CLASSIC
designs

Combine the empire-style elegance of traditional motifs, such as a wreath or fleur-de-lis, with the speed and ease of spray paints to give a room a complete new look with a distinct touch of class.

A large stenciling project, such as a pattern of stripes and motifs above a chair rail, is less time-consuming if you use spray paint. Although less economical than acrylic stencil paints, spray paint is very speedy for covering large areas and creates some lovely effects.

Adapting stencils

Make the most of the motifs by extending the border to create a long strip, or turn the two halves of the wreath into a wave border by stenciling the two halves alternately in a long chain. Use the fleur-de-lis as a classic decoration on accessories, such as lampshades, cushions, trinket boxes or book covers.

Wreaths

Use this design as a complete wreath—or adapt it to make two separate leafy curves and create a striking linked effect to decorate a painted dado line.

4 Stencil in three colors

● Start by dabbing dark brown over the first part of the stencil. Continue with light brown for the middle area of the leaves, overlapping the brown slightly to blend the colors. Complete the motif with gold, blending it into the light brown.

3 Prepare the wall

● Mark off a line at chair-rail height and mask at this level all around the room. Paint the area above the tape in cream and allow to completely dry. Remask along the edge of the cream area to reveal the lower half of the wall. Paint this in a contrasting color.

YOU WILL NEED:
● Wreath stencil
● 1-oz bottle water-based stencil paint in beige, brown and gold
● Household sponge or foam sponge
● Masking tape
● Scissors
● Stencil acetate
● Fine permanent marker
● Cutting mat
● Craft knife
● Mixing palette

5 Build the design

● Position the second stencil above the dado line so that the stem just abuts the end leaf of the first half-wreath and the end leaf just meets the line. Blend the colors as before and continue around the room, using one stencil for all the top motifs and the other for all the bottom motifs.

● Starting from one corner of the wall, attach the stencil below the dado line so that the tip of the stem and the end of the top leaf sit on the dividing line.

1 Trace the design

● Tape a piece of stencil acetate over one half of the wreath stencil, allowing at least 1¼" space on all sides. Using a fine marker, trace around the outline of one half of the wreath. Repeat with another piece of acetate to make a copy of the other half of the wreath, filling in the broken section of the stem by hand.

2 Cut the stencils

● Place the traced motifs on the cutting mat and cut out the designs with a knife.

6 Finish the dado

● Continue along the wall. If there is any space at the end, press a ruler into the corner over the stencil so that it bends with the angle. Tape both sides of the stencil in place and color both sides of the motif, holding a piece of cardboard on one side as a mask while stenciling the other side.

Fleur-de-lis

The fleur-de-lis—a classic stylized iris, which is the traditional heraldic emblem of the kings of France—will add a regal touch when used to decorate fabrics, accessories or other items, such as this corner cupboard.

TIPS

■ When drawing a perfect horizontal line around the room to follow as a dado between two different colors, use the same trick as for marking the diagonals of the cupboard door panel. Mark points the same height from the floor at both ends of each wall, attach a length of chalked string at one mark and fix it firmly to the other mark. Twang the string for a perfect horizontal.

YOU WILL NEED:

(plus gold and brown, optional)
- Gold stencil crayons
- Stencil brush
- Household sponge or foam sponge pieces
- Masking tape
- String and chalk
- Palette

- Fleur-de-lis from the Stencil Collection
- 1-oz bottle water-based stencil paint in red

2 Align the motif

● Position the fleur-de-lis stencil so that the point where the two outer petals join fits exactly into the intersection of the chalk lines. Tape it firmly in place as close as possible to the motif, keeping the stencil flush with the panel.

■ If you use spray adhesive to fix your stencils in place, put the stencil in a large box before you spray it—this minimizes the sticky particles that linger in the air.

■ If you want to intersperse your stenciled rope columns with wreath motifs for an allover wallpaper effect, as shown on pages 160-1, you will need to plan the positioning carefully before you start.

1 Mark the center

● Attach a length of string to one corner of the central panel and chalk the string to coat it. Attach the other end taut to the opposite corner and secure in place. Snap the string to create a diagonal chalk line. Repeat to add the other diagonal.

3 Stencil the base color

● Pick up a little red stencil paint on a piece of sponge, wipe off the excess and dab evenly over the fleur motif. Blend with gold and brown, if you choose. Allow this to dry completely before adding the shading, as this is oil-based and will not mix with the water-based paint if wet.

4 Add gold highlights

● Break the seal on the end of a gold oil-based stencil crayon and pick up color from the tip on a stencil brush. Dab this lightly over one side of the stencil to give a shaded highlight. Don't be tempted to apply the stencil crayon directly to the design—the effect is thick and unsubtle.

5 Remove the chalk

● Remove the stencil and allow the gold color to dry. Rub off the chalk lines with a slightly damp cloth. Add any finishing touches, such as a masked border around the inside of the panel, if you wish.

Outline on fabric

● Rather than filling in the motif with solid color, use the fleur-de-lis stencil to create an outline to decorate fabrics or accessories.

Fabric markers

● Make sure your fabric is laid out taut, attach the stencil, then use a gold fabric pen to draw in the outline of the windows.

Rope border

Extend and repeat the motif to make a long strip for columns and borders.

1 Mark lines

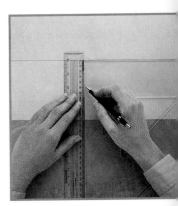

● On a long piece of stencil acetate, rule a line across the top of a set square at least 4" in from the edge of the acetate. Measure points 1 ¾" from the line at right angles and rule in a second line to join the marked points.

EQUIPMENT.

YOU WILL NEED:
● **Classic stencils from the Stencil Collection**
● **Six 12-oz cans spray paint in white**
● **Large sheet of stencil acetate**
● **Ruler and set square**
● **Fine pencil**
● **Cutting mat**
● **Craft knife**
● **Plumb line**
● **Masking tape**
● **Scissors**
● **Large sheets of brown paper**
● **Spray adhesive**
The above quantities will cover the area above a chair rail in a 6' x 18' hall.

2 Mark the repeats

● Place the rope stencil over the acetate so that it sits evenly inside the drawn lines. With a pencil or very fine permanent marker, draw closely around the inside of the stencil. Reposition and repeat the design along the length of acetate until you have a long but still manageable strip.

3 Cut the stencil

● Place the traced design on a cutting mat and using a craft knife, cut out the marked windows (see Cutting Your Own Stencil, p 137). Leave the drawn lines on as guide for positioning.

4 Planning

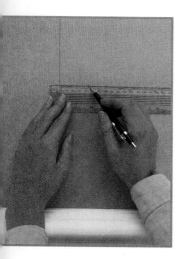

● Drop a plumb line from the point on the cornice where you want to stencil your first stripe. Draw a line perpendicular to the chair rail. Repeat 1 ¾" away to make a guideline. Repeat these column guidelines all around the room, leaving a space 12" wide between each pair of lines.

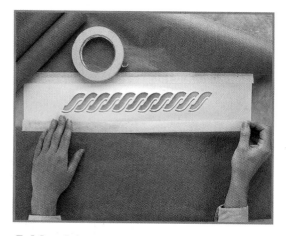

5 Masking

● Spray paint tends to drift beyond the edges of the stencil, so protect your wall by masking around the stencil. Attach a wide border of brown paper around all edges of the stencil with masking tape.

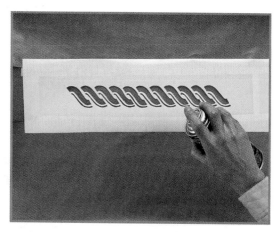

6 Spray-on adhesive

● In a well-ventilated room, place the masked stencil on newspaper or a drop cloth and spray adhesive over the back of the stencil to the edges of the acetate. Hold the can at arm's length and avoid inhaling the spray as you work.

Take great care when using both spray adhesive and spray paint that you do not inhale the mist of tiny particles that spraying creates. Work in a well-ventilated room, try to spray within a contained area, such as a large box, and if you are doing a lot of spraying, wear a face mask for added protection.

7 Spraying

● Position the stencil exactly inside the first set of guidelines and fix in place, attaching the brown paper to the wall with masking tape. Following the manufacturer's instructions, spray over the stencil in light strokes—heavy spraying will make the paint run. Remove the stencil, and for speed, use a hair dryer to dry the paint before stenciling the next strip.

● To add the wreath motif to the design, see Tips, page 159 for planning and spacing.

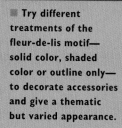 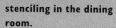

IDEAS

● **Use lengths of the rope border motif** as a decoration for upholstery, as shown above. The angled shape at the end of each *S* shape makes it ideal for linking to form squares and diamond shapes.

● Try different treatments of the fleur-de-lis motif—solid color, shaded color or outline only—to decorate accessories and give a thematic but varied appearance.

● For a special occasion, stencil table napkins—either fabric or paper—or other accessories to match

stenciling in the dining room.

● Trim a shelf by stenciling a continuous strip of the rope motif in shaded colors that match your room. The repeating pattern lends itself perfectly to use as borders, trims, columns or as a faux panel effect on a plain door.

This Flower Posy stencil—
an abundance of cottage
garden flowers, freshly
gathered and tied with a
bow—makes a delightful
addition to your collection.
Whether you prefer a wash
of natural colors or a single
pretty shade, the posy
brings a touch of summer
to your home.

Flower posy

YOU WILL NEED:

- Flower Posy from the Stencil Collection
- 1-oz bottles of water-based stencil paint in white and six other colors
- Household sponge or foam sponge pieces
- Fine artist's brush
- Palette
- Masking tape
- Scissors

Give your fabrics and furnishings a pretty, coordinated look with the Flower Posy stencil from the Stencil Collection. This lovely bouquet makes an ideal motif for use individually on accessories such as lampshades or fire screens, as a coordinating device on cupboard doors or dining chairs or with areas masked off to form a chain, a frieze or a flower wreath.

The assorted blooms in the posy give you endless options for colorways. You can tint each flower individually in brilliant shades to give a riot of color or keep them subtle with a selection of pretty pastels. Or you could apply a single color to the stencil in a shade slightly darker than your background to give a simple, monochrome look.

You can use some stencil paints on fabrics, if you don't expect to wash them often (check the manufacturer's instructions), but on items such as cushion covers, it is safer to use fabric paints. If you are coordinating fabrics with walls, make sure you choose a range of colors that is available in both fabric and standard paints.

Planning

If you are using a range of colors to stencil your posy, it's a good idea to experiment first with different combinations. If you decide to stencil on fabric, test the colors on a scrap of the same material to see how they take (when the paint is dry, wash the fabric gently to see if the paints are colorfast). When you are happy with your colors, gather your equipment and prepare your paints in a palette.

The stencil

For a crisp, fresh look to your stencil, each bloom should be masked individually before you apply the color. For a more shaded effect, the flowers can be left unmasked, with one color stenciled straight after another to give a rainbow feel. The bow, however, should be masked off before stenciling to maintain its sharply defined edge.

1 Mask the bow

● Cover the stencil bow with masking tape to ensure that no stray colors are sponged over it while you stencil the posy. Center the motif on a chair back and secure with masking tape.

2 Start to stencil

● Using a small section of sponge with your first stencil color, dab a fine layer of paint over the left-hand side of the rose. Keep the tone strong on the outer petals, but gradually fade the shade as you work toward the center of the flower head.

3 Change colors

● Use a fresh piece of sponge with your second color and dab it across the right-hand side of the rose, keeping a small, paint-free area between the two different shades.

4 Blend the two colors

● Dab a third piece of dry sponge over the two colors while they are still wet, blending them well to create a graduated tone from one to the other. If your surface is particularly absorbent, you may need a quick touch-up of each color before you sponge them together—but be sparing with the paints, or the result will be an unsightly splotch rather than a delicate shading.

TIPS

5 Stencil the remaining flowers

● Take a clean piece of sponge for each new color and stencil the rest of the flowers, blending the colors slightly where they meet.

● Finish the posy by filling in the flower stalks below the bow. With multi-colored flowers, use a plain shade or a two-tone green.

IDEAS

■ Pick one individual flower, such as the rose, the sunflower or the bud, and stencil it as an additional motif to accompany the posy. Place the flower at all four corners of the design or use it to embellish surrounding furnishings. For example, you could use the posy as a frieze on a tablecloth, and the single rose to create coordinating napkins.

■ Use the stencil upside down and color it with muted tones to resemble a hanging bunch of dried flowers.

■ Paint or stencil a scattering of petals around the outside of the posy. This will enlarge the finished design and create a feeling of gentle movement in a wafting summer breeze.

■ Create a pretty motif above a vase that stands flush against the wall on a display shelf—mask off the stalks and bow, then stencil your posy just above the vase to give a trompe l'oeil effect. Alternatively, stencil the posy on the wall at the back of the shelf and paint a vase in freehand underneath.

6 Peel off the stencil

● Once you are satisfied that the paint is dry, loosen all but one corner of the masking tape and peel back the stencil. Check that you are happy with your design. If you want to add any additional colors or strengthen the definition of a particular flower, replace the stencil and work over those areas again.

PHOTOGRAPHY BY LUCINDA SYMONS

7 Mask around the bow

● Peel off the masking tape covering the bow area, then cut further strips of tape and mask off the flower heads and stalks all around the edges of the bow.

8 Reposition the stencil

● Replace the stencil in the same position as before and tape to the back of the chair.
● If you are using the stencil diagonally, you can adjust the position of the bow to hang down toward the ground. Stencil the bow in a dark color so that it will cover any overlap of the flowers or stems. If you are using the motif upside down, position the stencil as usual, but mask off the two bow tails so that they don't appear to hang against gravity.

9 Stencil the bow

● Work the bow in a strong, contrasting shade, building up the color gradually to give real depth. Allow the paint to dry, then shade the bow with a fine stipple of white, silver or gold paint to give the ribbon a three-dimensional appearance. When you are satisfied, peel off the stencil to reveal the completed design.

CHAPTER 4

How To

YOU WILL NEED:
- ● Latex paint
- ● Paintbrush or roller
- ● All-purpose primer
- ● Flexible putty knife
- ● Spackling compound or joint compound
- ● Bowl or hawk to hold joint compound
- ● Fine-grade sandpaper
- ● Sanding block or power sander
- ● Dust mask
- ● Self-adhesive joint tape
- ● Paintable caulking
- ● Caulking gun
- ● Utility knife

Repairing CRACKED

The wall and ceiling surfaces in older homes will almost certainly be finished with plaster to create a surface suitable for decorating. Today's solid plaster walls are usually finished with a two-coat system—a thick undercoat and a thinner finish with a total thickness of about ½". In older homes, the plaster is generally thicker; a three-coat system was the norm. Alternatively, the walls and ceilings may have been lined with vertical wood battens and closely spaced horizontal wood laths over which the plaster was spread; this type of wall will sound hollow when tapped. Ceilings and walls in newer homes are clad with sheets of drywall (also called wallboard or sheetrock), and sometimes covered with a thin finishing coat of joint compound.

What can go wrong

As time goes by, both plaster and drywall can develop surface cracks—small hairline cracks or larger, deeper cracks—caused either by slight movement of the house structure or by something colliding with the surface. Accidental damage affects drywall and lath-and-plaster surfaces more drastically than those with plaster on solid masonry. Whatever the problem, you need to restore the surface to its original pristine condition before you decorate it. Here is what to do.

Using spackling compound

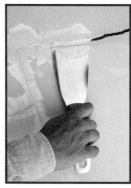

▲ Cracks in old plaster

● If the surface has only a mass of tiny hairline cracks, the best way of filling them is to apply a coat of latex paint. Work it well into the surface using a brush or roller so that the paint bridges the cracks. If the plaster has not been painted and seems very porous—soaking up water immediately if you splash some on it—then treat it with a coat of all-purpose primer. This will reduce and even out the porosity and provide the perfect base for a painted finish.

● If the plaster has larger cracks, you must fill them one by one. Start by raking out all the loose material with the corner of your putty knife, angling it so you undercut the edges of the crack slightly; this allows the filler to bond better to the plaster. Then brush or blow away any remaining dust.

● Moisten the crack with a wet paintbrush, then apply a prepared spackling compound. Press the spackling

Using paintable caulking

Cracks between walls

Slight movement can often open up slight cracks between adjacent walls or between walls and ceilings on new plaster. Similarly, drywall ceilings and walls often develop long, straight cracks along the board joints if they were not taped when they were installed. The ideal material for filling these is paintable caulking, which will not crack or fall out if future movement occurs between the boards or wall surfaces. The caulking comes in large cartridges, and you will need to apply it using a caulking gun.

● To prepare cracks between walls and ceilings or in the angle between two walls, use your putty knife to rake out loose material, as described for preparing cracks in old plaster. Brush along the cracks with an old paintbrush to remove any remaining dust, then wet down the plaster.

● Use a utility knife to cut the end of the nozzle on the cartridge at an angle of about 45° to give a bead slightly wider than the crack, and pipe some caulking along it. Hold the nozzle at 45° to the surface and push it away from you so that the nozzle shapes the bead neatly as it is extruded from the nozzle.

● Moisten your finger and use it to smooth the caulking along the joint line. You should aim to leave a smooth, concave bead in the angle. Allow a surface skin to form before you paint over it.

● For cracks between pieces of drywall, apply the caulking, using the gun in the same way and overfilling slightly, then draw your putty knife along the crack to leave the caulking perfectly flush with the drywall surface. Allow a surface skin to form before painting over the caulking.

● Alternatively, stick self-adhesive joint tape along the crack, smoothing it well toward the edges, as for repairing holes in drywall, then apply a thin layer of joint compound over it. Sand as for a filled crack.

Damaged drywall

To patch a hole in drywall, clean away any surface fibers, pressing them back into the hole, then cover the hole with one or more pieces of self-adhesive joint tape, smoothing and pressing it down firmly from the hole outward toward the edges of the tape. (This specially designed mesh tape is also good for repairing cracks—it is designed to press down so that the edges do not stand proud of the surface you are repairing.)

● Spread joint compound over the tape and smooth it out, feathering the edges on the surrounding surface, to leave an almost imperceptible repair. Sand down as for a filled crack.

PLASTER

compound well into the crack by drawing your putty knife first across the crack line (as in the photo, left), then along it. Aim to leave the spackle slightly proud of the surrounding surface.

● If the crack is deeper than about ⅛", fill it with joint compound in stages; allow each layer to set before adding the next. If you try to fill in one layer, the compound may pull out of the crack and will itself crack as it dries.

● When the compound has set hard, sand it

smooth to be flush with the surrounding plaster, using fine sandpaper. Wrap the sandpaper around a sanding block if you have only a few cracks to deal with; use an orbital (finishing) power sander to tackle larger areas. Use the vacuum cleaner attachment if your sander has one;

Larger holes

● Patch larger holes in the plaster on solid walls by brushing out loose material, wetting the plaster surface and then filling the hole in layers no more than about ⅛" thick (as above). Let each layer harden before applying the next one and finish by slightly overfilling the hole so that you can sand it down flush with the surrounding plaster when it has dried.

otherwise, wear a dust mask so that you do not inhale the fine dust that this produces.

Lath and plaster

▶ ● Patch damage to lath-and-plaster walls by removing all the cracked plaster. Brush away any dust and if

the hole is very large, press hardware cloth or crumpled newspaper into it so that the spackling compound will adhere and to prevent it from dropping down into the wall cavity.

● Wet the edges of the area and any exposed laths and force spackle into the hole so it is squeezed between the laths. Build up the repair in stages as for larger holes, overfilling the hole. Sand down as for a crack.

Whatever you want to paint—from something as small as a tray to a surface as large as a paneled wall, you need to prepare the existing finish so that it will be suitable to take the type of paint you want to use.

Apart from walls, the surfaces you are most likely to want to paint and renovate or redecorate are wooden or laminated pieces of furniture, and these need to be prepared in keeping with the existing surface and the type of finish you want to give them. For example, if you want to change the finish from an oil-based paint to a water-based one, it is important to prepare the surface correctly to get a good and lasting finish. So never skimp or improvise on preparation—it is the key to a good result.

Preparing furniture

You may acquire furniture, both new and second-hand, that you want to repaint or restore—and in each case, you need to prepare the surface according to the existing finish and the way you want to paint it.

New wood

New, unfinished wood needs preparation before you can paint it. If there are cracks, fill these with wood putty, as for repairing wood surfaces (see page 172). Sand the surface until smooth with fine sandpaper, wipe clean, then follow the steps on the right.

Before yo

1 If the wood has surface knots, you need to treat these with a shellac-based sealer to prevent sap from seeping through and staining the painted finish. Using a small brush, paint sealer over the knots as shown on the left and allow to dry—this takes about an hour.

2 Treat the new wood all over with an oil- or water-based primer, according to the paint you wish to use. As a rule of thumb, use an oil-based primer for oil-based paint and a water-based primer for latex and acrylic paints. Dilute the primer with a little paint thinner or water, according to its base.

3 Apply one coat of your chosen paint and allow it to dry completely. Sand the surface lightly with fine sandpaper, then wipe clean before applying the second coat.

4 To protect a completely flat finish from dirt and damage, cover the paintwork with dead-flat matte varnish. You will need to stir this well to incorporate the chalk but do not shake it, as that will introduce air bubbles, which are hard to disperse. For finishes with a slight sheen, use an appropriate oil- or water-based varnish for the surface.

Removing ol

Waxed furniture

1 **To make a waxed surface suitable for painting, wipe over with paint thinner, as for oil-based finishes, above.**

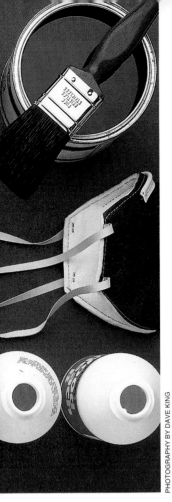

PHOTOGRAPHY BY DAVE KING

EQUIPMENT

SELECT WHAT YOU NEED FROM THE FOLLOWING:

- Wood putty
- Fine-grade sandpaper
- Shellac-based sealer
- Oil- or water-based primer
- ½" paintbrush
- 1 ½" or 2" paintbrush
- Dead-flat matte varnish
- Lint-free cloth
- Paint thinner
- Shellac
- Fine-grade steel wool
- Heat gun paint stripper
- Rotary wire paint stripper
- Wood bleach
- Firm brush
- Dust mask
- Heavy-duty gloves
- Quick-strip stripper
- Liquid paint stripper

u paint

Sound oil-based finishes

If the surface of a piece of used furniture is in reasonably good condition, it may have an oil-based finish, and you will need to prepare it for painting accordingly.

1 Dampen a lint-free cloth with paint thinner; wipe over the surface to clean it thoroughly.

2 Paint over the whole surface with shellac to seal. As for flat varnish, you will need to stir the shellac well to mix it, but avoid shaking it so as not to incorporate bubbles. Allow to dry—this will take about an hour.

3 The shellac forms an impermeable barrier between the old finish and the new one, so you can now use a water-based paint on the surface without fear of the oil-based layer spoiling the fresh water-based finish.

Stained wood

■ Even though you have stripped wood back to its bare surface, it may have been stained. The only way to remove this coloring is by using wood bleach, which is very caustic and needs to be handled with care.

The bleach often comes as a two-part process that should be applied according to the maker's instructions.

■ Place the furniture on

protective paper and wearing a dust mask and gloves, paint the first solution over the wood. Leave for 10–20 minutes, then coat with the second solution. Leave in a well ventilated room for 3–4 hours.

■ Scrub the bleach out of the wood with a firm brush and water, as shown above. Rinse well and dry before treating and repainting as for new wood, left.

...ishes

2 Rub with fine steel wool to break up the surface. Wipe again with paint thinner.

3 Treat with shellac and paint, as for oil-based finishes.

Damaged wood

Fill minor cracks in wood with wood putty and rub down, as for preparing wood surfaces (see page 172). Rub down, then treat the surface according to the existing finish. If a piece of wooden furniture is badly damaged, you will need to strip it right back to the wood and start again. If you have a heat gun, use it to remove the paint or varnish, but be sure never to use this near glass. Otherwise, use a rotary wire paint stripper or one of the following traditional methods.

Painted or varnished furniture

For solid wood furniture, dip the whole piece in quick-strip paint stripper. This is not suitable for veneered surfaces, as it will dry and warp the wood. Instead, use a liquid paint stripper, following these steps:

1 Place the furniture on plenty of paper so that drops of stripper cannot burn your

flooring. Wearing goggles, a dust mask and heavy rubber gloves, brush paint stripper evenly over the whole surface. Work in a well ventilated room and wash off any stripper that comes into contact with your skin immediately with water.

2 Allow stripper to work for 10–20 minutes, according to manufacturer's instructions, until the paint or varnish starts to bubble.

3 For flat areas, use a paint scraper, and for detailed or curved surfaces, use a wire brush to remove the dissolved paint. If necessary, reapply the stripper to deal with thick coatings.

4 Wipe the surface with a damp cloth, removing traces of stripper or dissolved paint. When the surface is clean and dry, sand well and treat as for new wood, left.

Preparing
WOODEN

FINE FURNITURE

YOU WILL NEED:

- Fine-grade sandpaper (for hand sanding or power sanding)
- Sanding block or orbital power sander
- Lint-free cloth
- Paint thinner
- Fine surface filler
- Putty knife
- Shellac-based sealer
- Paintbrush
- Wood primer
- Undercoat
- Oil-based paint
- Varnish
- Fine wet-and-dry sandpaper
- Wood putty
- All-purpose cleaner or household detergent
- Chemical paint stripper or heat gun
- Paint scraper
- Hammer and nails
- Screwdriver and screws
- Nail set
- Floor sander and belt sander (from rental shop)
- Hardboard plus nails or adhesive

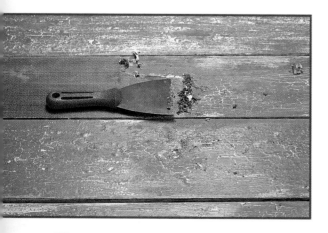

There are various wooden surfaces around the home that you might like to transform or personalize with decorative paint techniques. First, there is the furniture, and then the functional woodwork around the house— doors and trim, chair rails and baseboards, windows, shutters and staircases. Finally there is the floor, which can be given a wide range of painted finishes.

Different wood types

Most wood used in the home is natural wood—usually it is softwood, but you may find hardwood in older buildings. Being a natural product, wood not only has natural flaws, such as splits and knots, it also can be attacked by termites and carpenter ants and if it is persistently damp, by rot.

Plywood is also commonly used around the house and for home furnishings as well. It is made by bonding a series of thin wood veneers together, giving the appearance of a natural wooden surface and as such it can suffer the same ills as natural wood. Particleboard and hardboard, on the other hand, are wholly reconstituted materials, made by simply bonding together wood chips or fibers into a board with a smooth surface and, in the case of hardboard, perfectly smooth edges. Moisture is their main enemy.

Both natural wood and man-made boards suffer from wear and tear, with their surfaces often suffering from dents, chips and scratches. The surface you want to decorate may also bear evidence of earlier do-it-yourself activity in the form of nail or screw holes and may already have a decorative finish that itself needs attention. Whatever surface you are planning to work on, careful preparation is the key to final success.

Preparing new wood

New wood usually has a machine-planed surface that is reasonably smooth to the touch. Plywood and other man-made boards should be flat and smooth; always check plywood carefully to ensure that there is no sign of rippling or lifting in the surface veneers.

1 If the wood has no visible faults, sand it smooth with fine sandpaper, working in the direction of the grain. Wrap the paper around a sanding block or use a power sander for large flat areas. Wipe off the fine dust with a clean lint-free cloth moistened with paint thinner.

2 For a painted finish, fill any cracks or open grain with fine surface filler, rubbing the filler down when it has set. Treat knots with a coat of shellac-based sealer to prevent sap from bleeding through the paint film. Then apply a coat of oil-based wood primer, an undercoat in a color appropriate to the finish you intend to apply and two coats of oil-based paint. Rub down the surface between coats with fine wet-and-dry sandpaper to ensure a perfectly smooth finish.

3 For a clear finish, fill any surface blemishes with wood putty. This is available in different colors to match popular wood shades and will take wood stain successfully. When the filler has hardened, rub down the filler and surrounding wood, as in step 1.

SURFACES

Preparing painted or varnished wood

Many decorative paint effects can be applied over an existing paint or varnish finish as long as this is in good condition.

1 Inspect the surface for signs of chipping, flaking or dents. If it is free from defects, wash it with an all-purpose cleaner or household detergent to remove dirt and grease, rinse it with clean water and allow it to dry. To prepare the surface, sand it with fine wet-and-dry sandpaper, used wet, and rinse off the resulting paint slurry with more clean water.

2 If the surface is chipped and exposes bare wood, fill it with wood primer and then undercoat to make the surface level. If the wood itself is dented, overfill the damage with wood putty and allow it to set hard. Then sand and seal the repair with undercoat, followed by a thinned coat of oil-based paint.

3 If the paint is flaking very badly, it is best to strip it completely. Use a chemical paint stripper for wood if you want a clear finish or are working on an intricately molded surface; use a heat gun for a painted finish. Then treat the stripped wood as described under Preparing New Wood, above.

Preparing floors

Preparation depends on the present condition of the floorboards. Particleboard floors offer a flatter, smoother surface than traditional tongue-and-groove or square-edged floorboards.

1 Take up existing floor coverings and inspect the boards, as they may have warped, shrunk or split. Unless fairly new, they are likely to be marked and there may be gaps between the boards.

2 Countersink all raised nails with a hammer and nail set so their heads are at least ⅛" below the board surface and fill the holes with wood putty. Hold down warped boards by fixing them with screws rather than nails. Replace badly damaged boards with new wood; you will have to split off the tongues with a sharp knife first to release tongue-and-groove boards.

3 Remove any wax polish before you apply a painted finish—a long scrubbing job. You may consider covering the boards with hardboard (see step 6).

4 Restore a sound but badly marked floor, using a rented floor sander and a belt sander to tackle the perimeter areas the floor sander will not reach. Work diagonally across the boards.

5 With the preparation completed, seal the board surface. Use wood primer, undercoat and two coats of oil-based paint as a base for painted effects, and clear varnish if you want the wood grain to remain visible—under a stenciled design, for example. If using a clear sealer, thin the first coat by adding 10 percent paint thinner to help it to penetrate the wood and bond well to the floor surface. Then add two or three full-strength coats.

6 In cases of severe damage or where there are gaps between boards, you can take a shortcut and cover the floor with hardboard sheets that provide a perfectly flat surface for paint effects. The boards can be nailed or glued in place; however, do not use adhesive if the boards may need to be lifted for underfloor work at a later date. Standard sheets are large (4' x 8'), but you can cut these into smaller panels (2' squares, for example) to create a decorative tiled effect. Seal the hardboard sheets as for bare wood (see step 5).

Varnishes & gla

Varnishes and glazes are essential elements in many decorative paint finishes. Varnish is generally used as a transparent protective finishing coat; glaze is a medium that is tinted with color and used to create the paint effect itself. Varnishes are widely available, but you may need a specialty supplier for glazes.

Oil-based varnishes are tough, extremely durable and slow drying; they require paint thinner or turpentine for thinning and cleaning. Water-based varnishes are easier to apply and clean, dry more quickly and will not yellow with age.

1 & 7 Polyurethane varnish An oil-based product, this finish is very hard-wearing and resistant to heat and alcohol. It takes 4–6 hours to dry and should be left overnight before recoating. Flat (matte), satin (mid-sheen) and high-gloss finishes are available in clear (see D, opposite) and pigmented types, or in stained varieties to use on natural wood to simulate the colors of different woods, such as dark mahogany (A), antique pine (B) and teak (C).

2 & 6 Acrylic varnish is water-based and dries in about an hour. It does not yellow with age like most oil-based varnishes, but is not as hard-wearing, so you need several coats. Available in flat, satin and gloss finishes and in clear or pigmented versions.

3 Scumble glaze is an opaque glaze, applied over a base coat; while wet, it is dragged with a comb or wiped with a rag, which removes portions of the scumble color. A satin-finish or flat alkyd paint, lightly thinned, can be used as a scumble. Add a touch of boiled linseed oil or kerosene to the alkyd paint to extend the working time of the scumble.

4 Crackle-glaze varnish is a speciality product used to create a surface finish with a cracked appearance. The name is applied loosely to two different types—one is used between two layers of water-based paint to crackle the upper layer, while the other is a two-coat varnish system where the quicker-drying top coat is applied over a slower-drying base coat.

5 Spray varnish is available in gloss, satin and flat finishes, in both oil-based and acrylic varieties, and is suitable for furniture or for retouching and protecting paintings. It is useful for decorating awkwardly shaped items but is expensive to use for large areas.

8 Traditional oil-based glazing liquid is a transparent medium, tinted with artist's oil colors and used for various paint effects, such as dragging. Paint thinner can be added to keep glaze workable, while a little raw linseed oil can help to retard drying. The glaze appears opaque in the can but dries to a transparent finish. Some glazes are noticeably yellow, so take care when using them with blue and gray pigments, which can turn slightly green as a result. Tinted glazes are available, but most decorators prefer to mix their own colors. Oil glaze has a low flash point, so keep it well away from open flames and dry out cloths soaked in glaze before throwing them away to avoid spontaneous combustion.

9 & 10 Oil-based varnish is the traditional clear wood finish, made with natural oils and resins dissolved in paint thinner. Available from specialty suppliers in various finishes, including satin (9) and dead flat (10).

11 Shellac is made by dissolving shellac or other resin in alcohol. It dries in 15 to 30

DAVE KING

1

2

3

4

5

zes

minutes to a hard but brittle surface film that is not resistant to water or alcohol. It is difficult to brush on, so is more often applied with a pad as a sealant over French-polished wood or between the base coat and the surface glaze for some paint effects. It does not keep well, so buy only what you need.

Also available:

Lacquer is a high-gloss finish used in the furniture trade to give a hard, durable finish. It dries almost instantly and is recommended for professional use only.

Alkyd varnish is solvent-based but tougher than traditional oil varnishes. It takes 4–6 hours to dry, and can be over-coated after about 12 hours. The finish can be flat, satin or high gloss, in pigmented and clear types. Modified types (marine or yacht varnish) are very durable, and are often used as wood-trim sealers.

Latex glazing liquid is a medium used as an alternative to oil-based glaze or as a protective finish. It dries very quickly, so it may not suit beginners; however, you can use an additive called an *extender* to lengthen the workable time of the glaze. It is not as tough as oil glaze but does not yellow with age. Available in flat, mid-sheen and gloss finishes, you can tint it with a colorant or add it to water-based paints for a translucent finish.

Tiles

It's easy to master the art of working with tiles if you learn the tricks the professionals use for cutting and fitting tiles on any surface.

Tiles are a popular finish for walls and floors. Aside from the wealth of decoration they provide, tiles appeal to the home decorator because their small size makes them far easier to work with than rolls of wallcoverings or sheet flooring. However, while tiling an unobstructed surface is easy, it takes more skill to deal with cutting tiles to fit around door and window openings, switches and outlets, radiators and heating ducts, especially when you are using ceramic tiles. Here's a look at the basics of successful tiling and at some of the tricks of the trade that you can use to deal with the tricky parts.

■ MARKING BORDER TILES

You can mark the width of border tiles in one of two ways. The first is by directly measuring the gap you need to tile, the second is to use two whole tiles to transfer the width of the border space onto the tile you are going to cut.

1 Place a loose whole tile on top of the last whole tile laid, then place a second tile on top with one edge touching the wall. Along the opposite edge of this tile, mark a line on the sandwiched tile and cut along the line. The exposed part of the sandwiched tile will fit perfectly into the border.

2 You can use the same trick to mark the L-shaped tile section needed to fit an external corner or around the edge of a door frame: Simply repeat the operation on each side of the corner in turn with the same tile sandwiched each time. The resulting intersecting lines give the L-shape required.

■ MEASURING AROUND BATHROOM ACCESSORIES

If you are making a backsplash, it makes sense to bring the tiles down around each side of the sink. In order to do this, however, you will need to accommodate the irregular shape. Use a contour gauge, which has thin adjustable rods that will mold around any shape you press it against, to make a traceable contour of the side of the sink.

1 Making sure the top of the contour gauge lies on a true horizontal, adjust it to follow the outline of the side of the sink (right). Place it over the tiles at the correct height and trace around the shape, using a china marker.

2 Using a tile cutter, cut along the guideline on each tile.

■ CUTTING TILES

When cutting ceramic tiles, you will get the best results if you cut the marked tile with a tile cutter or score the tile with a glass cutter, using a straightedge.

1 To cut resilient floor tiles, use a sharp utility knife and a steel ruler, and work on a cutting mat. Always draw the knife blade away from the hand holding the tile, so that a slip will not cause an accident.

SELECT WHAT YOU NEED FROM THE FOLLOWING:

- Ceramic wall tiles
- Cork floor tiles
- Ceramic floor tiles
- Vinyl floor tiles
- Trim tiles
- Tile cutting jig
- Tile cutter
- Tile saw
- Contour gauge
- Ceramic tile grout and adhesive
- Notched trowel
- Cork tile adhesive
- Vinyl tile adhesive
- Gauge stick
- Wooden battens
- Black marking pen
- Pencil
- Spirit level
- Plumb line
- Common nails
- Masonry nails
- Hammer
- String
- Chalk
- Tape measure
- Ruler
- Glass cutter
- Cutting mat
- Plastic corner strip
- China marker
- Scissors

Tiling walls

Achieving professional-looking tiling depends on two factors: positioning the tiles carefully and working to a true horizontal—not necessarily the baseboard.

Positioning involves selecting a starting point so that the tile layout is centered on the wall, with cut pieces of equal size at the end of each row and of each column, if the tiling is full height. This is easy on a plain wall, but harder if there are door and window openings to accommodate. The solution is to make a gauge stick—a length of wood marked off in tile widths. Hold it against the wall in various positions to see how the tiles will fall and adjust your starting point to get the best compromise between centering the layout and avoiding narrow cut tiles.

Once you have centered the layout, mark a horizontal guideline in line with the bottom edge of the lowest row of whole tiles; attach a wooden batten to the wall at this level. This will ensure that each row is horizontal. Secure it with partially driven nails, then remove to fit the bottom row of cut tiles.

Tiling floors

Tiling the floor is simpler than tiling walls, as you can lay rows of dry tiles and move them around to get the best layout, before you actually start laying them.

First, find the center of the room by joining the midpoints of opposite walls with string lines. In rooms that are not rectangular, use the midpoints of the two longest adjacent walls to establish the center. Lay a row of tiles from the center outward to check the width of the perimeter gap. If this is less than a quarter of a tile wide, remove a tile from the row and recenter the row across the room. If the gap is more than three-quarters of a tile wide, add a tile to the row. Mark the starting point, and you are ready to tile.

If you are laying resilient tiles—cork or vinyl—cover the floorboards with hardboard first to prevent the board edges from showing through. Nail at 6" intervals at the edges and across the center of the sheets.

If you are laying ceramic or quarry tiles on a boarded floor, cover it with sheets of $\frac{5}{8}$"-thick exterior-grade plywood first, to eliminate the risk of the tiles cracking as the floor moves. Screw into place.

Tiling over openings

If you are fitting tiles over a door or window, use a wooden batten to support the lowest row of whole tiles on the wall above. Remove it when the adhesive has set, then fit the cut tiles below. If you are tiling the underside of a door or window jamb, fit a plastic corner strip to the angle and complete the wall tiling. Press the tiles into adhesive on the underside of the jamb and prop them up with a shim wedged in place with a wooden batten. Remove when the adhesive has set.

2 To make small notched cutouts to fit around pipes and electrical fittings, use either a special tile saw to cut the tile or use a carbide-tipped hole saw to abrade it away. Nibbling out the waste area with nippers is a time-consuming, often inaccurate process that can result in a broken tile. If possible, slip the cut edge of a tile behind the switch or outlet cover plate and replace the existing screws with longer screws so that the cover plate fits over the tile edges.

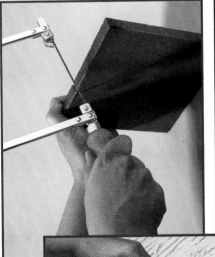

■ EXTERNAL CORNERS

When ceramic tiles had glazed edges, external corners were formed by overlapping the edges. Now most tile edges are unglazed, and so you need to use trim tiles or a plastic corner strip, set in the tile adhesive, to give a neat finish.

1 Where a corner is vertical, it looks best if whole tiles start each row on either side of the corner, especially if the tiles are patterned.

2 Where a corner is horizontal, such as at a window sill, you are likely to have a row of cut tiles immediately below the sill. Use whole tiles along the front edge of the sill to line up with those on the sides of the window jamb; fill in with cut tiles behind them.

3 With other tile types, use trim tiles or fit narrow wood trim or plastic molding over external corners to help protect the vulnerable tile edges from wear.

Water-based paints

Dilute the paint and clean brushes with water. Prime where necessary with water-based primer.

Type of paint	FLAT LATEX PAINT	SATIN-FINISH LATEX PAINT	SATIN-FINISH ACRYLIC PAINT
Suitable surfaces	Walls, ceilings, old and new plaster, brick. Do not use on metal.	More suited to walls than woodwork	Interior walls, wood or any smooth, sound surface
Primer	Prime, if using over bare plaster	Prime, if using over bare plaster or wood	Does not always need undercoat
Drying time	2–4 hours	2–4 hours	2–4 hours
Comments	Too absorbent for most decorative finishes but a good base for stenciling. Avoid using in steamy bathrooms—will soil, if not flat varnished.	A quick-drying paint, harder-wearing than flat latex paint, that gives a good finish to textured wallpapers.	A smooth, hard, opaque finish with a dull sheen between gloss and flat. A good base for decorative paint finishes but can be expensive.

Oil-based paints

Dilute the paint and clean brushes with paint thinner or mineral spirits. Prime where necessary with oil-

Type of paint	UNDERCOAT	SATIN-FINISH (MID-SHEEN)	LOW-LUSTER ENAMEL	FLAT ALKYD PAINT
Suitable surfaces	Walls and ceilings	Any smooth sound surface—walls or wood	Wood and metal	Walls and ceilings
Primer	Use appropriate primer if working on bare, unfinished surfaces.	Does not always need undercoat. Use primer on bare surfaces.	Use undercoat on new wood and metal primer on new metal.	Needs undercoat
Drying time	8–12 hours	12–16 hours	16 hours	6–12 hours
Comments	A good substitute for flat paint. Cheap, easy to apply; can be tinted for variety. Needs a coat of protective varnish.	Attractive soft-sheen finish. Covers well, is durable and washable and ideal as a base for decorative techniques.	Gives a softer sheen than gloss but is as durable as traditional gloss. Has some yellowing over time.	Has a perfectly flat finish but can show scuff marks. Often hard to obtain, it can be substituted with undercoat.

paints

Whatever you paint—from walls and ceilings to furniture or accessories—there is a paint that is just right for the job. Use this handy chart to ensure that you make the right choice.

TEXTURED PAINT

Walls and ceilings

Apply primer only on untreated surfaces.

4–8 hours, depending on thickness

Use to disguise uneven or weak surfaces. The textured finish is hard to wash and very difficult to remove.

HIGH-GLOSS LATEX PAINT

Interior woodwork and furniture

Apply ordinary primer and undercoat.

2–6 hours

Has the advantages of water-based paint, with the appearance and easy-cleaning qualities of gloss paint; not as durable as oil-based gloss.

WOOD WASH

Interior woodwork and furniture

Needs no undercoat. Seal new wood before wood-washing.

Less than half an hour

Easy to apply. Use as a stain or paint, giving several coats to build up depth of color.

COLOR WASH

Walls and ceilings, including painted wallpaper

Needs a sealer only if used on bare plaster.

1–4 hours

Available ready-mixed in water-based medium; otherwise, use 1:5 dilution of latex paint to water. Has an attractive transparent finish.

Shellac

This useful, denatured alcohol-based sealant comes in different "cuts," or grades, that vary in finish; the hardest of these is de-waxed shellac. Sand-and-seal shellac is specially formulated as a primer, but you can use regular shellac as a sealant for bare plaster or as an impermeable protective barrier between oil- and water-based paints on furniture and woodwork. The slightly chalky suspension needs to be stirred well before use, but avoid shaking it as this will introduce air bubbles, which are hard to disperse.

d primer.

GLOSS AND SEMIGLOSS

Wood and metal

Needs undercoat and if used on porous or new wood, primer too.

12–16 hours

Dries to a good sheen that is washable and resistant to dirt but can show up even small flaws on the surface.

ENAMEL PAINTS

Metal

Needs primer

12–16 hours

Hard-wearing washable finish that, unless applied carefully, will show up any flaws. Build up with several thin coats.

Specialty

There is a specialty brush tailor-made to create every imaginable effect, and the more adventurous you get with paint techniques, the more specialized brushes you will need. But you do not need to start off with a big selection—find out which brushes are invaluable, marked ***; which you can improvise, marked **; and which are a luxury, marked *.

1 TUFTED FAN GRAINER *
These splayed bristles add texture to paint and glaze finishes. Because the bristles are graduated in length, getting shorter toward the outer edges, they produce different impressions, creating delicate, graduated patterns.

2 FITCH LINER **
This firm-bristled brush gives even, straight lines when using glazes or oil paints and also because of its angled end, it is suitable for spattering techniques.
(A toothbrush, deftly used, is an ideal substitute for spattering at a fraction of the price).

3 SWORD STRIPER **
This hair brush with an angled tip was originally used just for painting perfect straight lines. Because of its soft, absorbent hair, it can create long even lines without needing to pause to pick up more paint. Today it is more commonly used for producing fine veins in marbling techniques.

4 OVERGRAINER *
This is a highly specialized brush, only for the really dedicated wood-graining enthusiast. The evenly spaced groups of bristles give soft-edged detail to fine, straight grain effects.

5 DUSTER GRAINING/GLAZING BRUSH **
These soft brushes were originally used completely dry for removing dust from surfaces to be painted. But today this is more commonly done with a cloth, so the duster brush is most useful as a softener for breaking down the distinct appearance of brushstrokes on glaze or for stippling in small areas.

6 TUFTED FAN GRAINER *
The large gaps between the clusters of this brush give a broken effect when adding texture to paint and glaze finishes. Although it gives interesting effects, this is a brush to treat yourself to when you have collected all the basics.

7 GRAINER/SCUMBLER *
This brush creates a textured, straight grain appearance when drawn through glaze. The two colors of bristles are of different textures, so when used together, the coarser of the two works between the softer bristles to give a texture of random lines.

8 ARTIST'S BRUSHES ***
It is important to have at least one soft artist's brush for correcting smudged edges of stenciling or touching up

brushes

paintwork in hard-to-reach details. They are available in sable or squirrel; if you buy only one, select a medium size, or pick several to give fine to thick lines.

9 LONG-HAIRED LINING BRUSH **

Not to be mistaken for an artist's brush, the ox hairs or sable hairs are too long to be controllable for ordinary painting but are ideal for making a thin flow of paint to give a long, fine line. Choose between this and a sword striper, depending on whether you most commonly want fine or medium-sized lines; use soft brushes for thin washes of paint and firmer brushes for thicker oil paints.

10 STIPPLER **

Stipplers are used to dab out the appearance of brushstrokes and to give a soft, speckled finish. To do this, you need to use a vertical dabbing motion—so the smaller the stippling brush you have, the longer a job will take to cover. (You can get a similar effect by using two 4" paintbrushes tied together.) The softest freckled effects come from using a pure bristle brush, but these are costly. You can use synthetic stipplers, but if you are only working on a small project, you get a softer effect if you use a duster brush in the same way.

11 ASSORTED FITCHES ***

Named after a member of the weasel family whose hairs used to be used to make these brushes, fitches are available thin, thick, pointed, flat, round or tapered and are used for small-scale and detailed work, such as adding knots on graining, or for freehand work on furniture. Nowadays fitches are made of densely packed white lily bristle, which holds a lot of paint and so makes them good for daubing, as well as for adding stippled detail in small corners. These are relatively inexpensive—choose one or two in different shapes for versatility.

12 BLENDER/SOFTENER **

Made of badger hair or hog hair, these soft natural brushes give a delicate clouded finish to marbling or wood-graining. The hog-hair brushes are less expensive than badger, but the bristles are less flexible, so the finished effect is not as soft. While these are tailor-made for softening and breaking down the glazework on graining, you can use a large, soft-bristled decorating brush with a very light touch. For marbling, however, you do need either a softener or duster brush for a professional finish.

13 STENCIL BRUSHES ***

These come in various sizes, made of different types of bristle. Although you can use a piece of foam sponge or cellulose sponge for stenciling, a brush is best for really fine color blending and for small areas of color with fine bridges. With careful cleaning, you can use a good stencil brush over and over again. Buy sizes 8, 12 and 14 to give a good range of size.

14 FLAT FITCH **

A flat hog bristle artist's brush; for uses see 11, above.

15 FLOGGER/DRAGGER **

Used to flick against wet glazework to create brushed patterns, these thin, horsehair brushes are also useful for dragging techniques, where the brush is laid almost flat against the surface and dragged through the glaze to give long, straight lines of textured color. You can imitate this effect with a long-bristled latex/acrylic brush, but the perfectionist should invest in either a flogger or a dragging brush.

SPECIAL EFFECTS
Equipment

The most exciting paint effects are created by texturing or manipulating the paint or glaze once it has been applied. These tools will help you create a variety of different styles and textures.

Apart from the enormous range of brushes, available from specialty suppliers, that are instrumental in many paint techniques, there is a selection of equipment—some very specialized items and some everyday household items—that is vital for effects such as marbling, wood-graining and combing. Most of this equipment is inexpensive, but if you decide to build up a collection of tools for a wide range of effects, you will find some items, such as the check roller, more costly.

1 Wax crayon

Although traditional techniques recommend that you use a feather and colored glaze for adding realistic veining to marbling, a more modern and, for beginners, much more controllable method is to use a dark wax crayon. The effect can be as distinct or as subtle as you like; follow the steps for marbling, starting on page 86, to take advantage of a very effective shortcut.

2 Veining feather

This is the traditional tool for veining marble, and you can not only add color to the effect but you can also use a feather to lift off or disperse tinted glaze while it is still wet to create lighter veins. The firm but flexible texture of a large turkey or goose feather is ideal for making continuous veins of smoothly varying width; with practice, you can trace veins as fine as a whisker or as thick as the side of your feather.

3 Rubber wood grainer

This heavy rubber wood-graining tool (also called *heart grainer*) is the forerunner of the rocker-type graining tool (4) and is used for creating the distinctive arched grains and knots of woods such as pine. Graining was traditionally an art that closely mimicked the colors and patterns of real wood, but today fantasy colors give the impression of fashionable wood staining or wood wash. Opt for the more durable model, the rocker-type graining tool (4), for easier cleaning and better-lasting qualities.

4 Rocker-type graining tool

With a reversible handle for heart-graining in upward and downward patterns, this graining tool has, in addition, two comb edges, the finer of which can be used for straight-graining. Rocker-type graining tools with a removable rubber face are available from decorative paint shops, specialty craft suppliers and by mail order.

5 a, b and c Steel graining combs

Available singly or in sets of up to 20, these combs come in a variety of widths with teeth of different thicknesses. Combed effects depend on drawing a comb edge through a tinted oil- or water-based glaze while it is still wet to reveal a

PHOTOGRAPHY BY DAVE KING

pattern in the background color. Although some techniques suggest covering steel combs with a thin cloth before using them, they can be used directly over wet glaze to give a very clear-edged design. For more details on combing, see pages 29–38.

6 Rubber grainer

This is used in the same way as a steel comb, but some are designed with wood effects in mind. This triangular grainer has faces with differently spaced teeth for straight pine and oak graining, and other rubber grainers are available with graduated teeth to give unusual patterns in simple combing. These are often made of black rubber, and you need to take care that the color does not come off on your work after the grainer has been in contact with paint thinner or oil color. You can make your own combs, using plastic (such as an old credit card) or cardboard and a craft knife (see page 32).

7 Natural sponge

The loose, springy texture of natural sea sponge is ideal for the techniques of sponging on or off, used over wet or dry paint or glaze. As these sponges are relatively expensive, it is important to clean them thoroughly before paint or glaze dries into the fibers. Rinse away any paint thinner or soap from cleaning and allow the sponge to dry where the air can circulate around it out of the way of direct heat.

8 Cheesecloth

Available in small packages from paint stores and in large bolts from hardware stores and decorative paint shops, cheesecloth is used for a variety of paint effects, including lifting off and softening the texture of paint or glaze in finishes such as marbling. Or buy cotton muslin or stockinette for an absorbent, lint-free cloth.

9 Household sponge

This springy, medium-textured sponge is very pliable and absorbent and is ideal for techniques such as color-washing, either with ready-mixed or homemade washes. This type of sponge is not suitable for sponging techniques, due to its

being more evenly textured than natural sponge, but it is possible to adapt a household sponge to give a soft, loose-textured print which is very like the effect of a natural one.

Synthetic sponges, with hard edges and a very close texture more like foam, are unsuitable for sponged effects, but are ideal for shaping for blocking or stamping.

10 Check or graining check roller

This roller has about 15 evenly spaced notched rotating discs, which create a broken effect. This tool was originally designed for use in wood-graining—by rolling it over a plain surface, it would make small indentations that would pick up deeper color when a glaze was applied. However, the tool creates an interesting effect in its own right; it is used, held firmly under a brush loaded with colored glaze (which coats the discs with color as they roll through), to produce an elegant broken grained effect.

11a, b and c Foam roller covers

Foam paint rollers are the basis for a huge range of inventive and clever effects, and all they need is a little adapting—tying with string or wire, binding, cutting or texturing—to create versatile patterns and stripes. Select the type of roller to suit the effect you want to create. If you want to produce distinct lines in your design, use an all-foam roller in a small or large size (a or c), bound or tied at intervals. For a close pattern, such as even lines of string texture, select a foam-coated roller with a solid core (b), for a much firmer base. For techniques and ideas with rollers, see Roller Tricks (pages 2–16).

5c

11c

11b

11a

8

7

10

9

BUYER'S GUIDE

Painting supplies and stenciling supplies are readily available at crafts shops, art supply stores and paint stores. Interior latex and oil-based paints and general painting supplies are carried by paint stores, home-improvement centers and hardware stores. Listed below is a sampling of mail-order sources that carry harder-to-find supplies and manufacturers to call for information.

Adele Bishop
3430 South Service Road
Burlington, Ontario
L7N3T9 Canada
800-510-0245
Catalog $4.00, refundable with first order.
Stencil paints, stencil supplies, stencil kits.

Benjamin Moore
51 Chestnut Ridge Road
Montvale, NJ 07645
888-236-6667. Call for nearest local retailer.
Complete line of interior and exterior paints, stains and varnishes.

Binney & Smith, Inc.
1100 Church Lane
P. O. Box 431
Easton, PA 18044-0431
800-272-9652. Call for nearest local retailer.
Artist's oil paints, acrylic paints.

Constantine's
2050 Eastchester Road
Bronx, NY 10461
800-223-8087
Free woodworker's catalog.
Plaster moldings and rosettes, antique-restoration supplies.

Delta Technical Coatings, Inc.
2550 Pellissier Place
Whittier, CA 90601
800-423-4135. Call for nearest local retailer.
Paint supplies, including stencil paint, acrylic paint, crackle medium, stains, finishes, glazing liquids.

Dick Blick
P. O. Box 1267
Galesburg, IL 61402-1267
800-447-8192
Catalog $5.00, refundable with first order.
Art supplies, including powder pigments, brushes, crackle medium, varnishes, fabric crayons, acrylic paints, acrylic mediums, artist's oil colors, adhesives, faux finishing kits, patina kits.

Duncan Enterprises
5673 E. Shields Avenue
Fresno, CA 93727
209-291-4444. Call for nearest local retailer.
Aleene's acrylic paints and mediums.

Janovic/Plaza
30-35 Thomson Avenue
Long Island City, NY 11101
800-772-4381
Catalog $4.95.
Specialty decorating supplies, including paints, graining combs, graining rollers, varnishes, sealers, glazing liquids, brushes.

Modern Options
2325 Third Street #339
San Francisco, CA 94107
415-252-5580. Call for nearest local retailer.
Free catalog.
Patina Antiquing Kit for verdigris finishing and faux patina supplies.

McCloskey Varnish Company
1191 South Wheeling Road
Wheeling, IL 60090
800-345-4530. Call for nearest local retailer.
Glazing liquids, wood stains.

Paint Effects
2426 Fillmore Street
San Francisco, CA 94115
415-292-7780
Web page:
www.painteffects.com
Formerly known as Paint Magic. Call or use web page to order.
Decorative painting and faux-finishing supplies, including pre-mixed glazes, crackle glazes, color-washing supplies.

Pearl Paint
308 Canal Street
New York, NY 10013-2572
Attn: Catalog Dept.
800-221-6845
Catalog $1.00.
Fine art, craft and graphic discount supplies, including artist's oil colors, powder pigments, acrylic paints, faux finish glazes, mediums, brushes, adhesives.

Plaid Enterprises, Inc.
1649 International Ct.
P. O. 7600
Norcross, GA 30091-7600
800-842-4197. Call for nearest local retailer.
Stencil supplies, acrylic paints, brushes, crackle medium, antiquing paint, glazes, graining combs.

Pottery Barn
P. O. Box 7044
San Francisco, CA 94120-7044
800-922-5507. Call for nearest local Decorator Store.
Paint Magic kits for faux finishes are available at Pottery Barn Decorator Stores around the country.

Sax Arts & Crafts
P. O. Box 510710
New Berlin, WI 53151-0710
800-558-6696
Catalog $5.00, refunded with first order; minimum order of $10.00.
Arts and crafts supplies, including artist's oil colors, artist's acrylic colors, powder pigments, stencil paint crayons, fabric crayons, brushes, mediums, palettes.

S&S Worldwide
P. O. Box 513
Colchester, CT 06415-0513
800-243-9232
Free catalog; minimum order of $25.00.
General arts and crafts supplies.

Sherwin-Williams Co.
101 Prospect Avenue
Cleveland, OH 44115-1075
800-474-3794. Call for nearest local retailer.
Complete line of interior and exterior paints and stains.

Thompson & Formby, Inc.
825 Crossover Lane
Memphis, TN 38117
800-367-6297. Call for nearest local retailer.
Wood stains, glazes, faux finishing kits.

United Gilsonite Laboratories
P. O. Box 70
Scranton, PA 18501-0070
800-272-3235
Free brochure.
Rocker-type graining tool (ZAR Graining Tool), wood stain.

INDEX